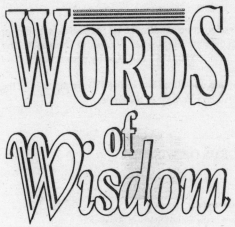

WORDS of Wisdom

For Daily Living

Charles H. Spurgeon

Whitaker House

Unless otherwise indicated, all Scripture quotations are from the *New King James Version*, © Thomas Nelson, Inc, 1979, 1980, 1982 and used by permission.

Scripture quotations marked (KJV) are taken from the *King James Version* of the Bible.

WORDS OF WISDOM

ISBN: 0-88368-368-7
Printed in the United States of America
Copyright © 1993 by Whitaker House

Whitaker House
580 Pittsburgh Street
Springdale, PA 15144

3 4 5 6 7 8 9 10 11 12 13 / 04 03 02 01 00 99 98 97 96 95

Contents

1

What Is Pride?

There is nothing into which the heart of man so easily falls as pride, and yet there is no vice which is more frequently, more emphatically, and more eloquently condemned in Scripture.

Pride is a *groundless thing*. It stands on the sands, or—worse than that—it puts its foot on the billows which yield beneath its tread. Even worse still, it stands on bubbles which soon must burst beneath its feet. Of all things, pride has the worst foothold. It has no solid rock on earth on which to place itself. We have reasons for almost everything, but we have no reasons for pride. Pride is a thing which should be unnatural to us, for we have nothing to be proud of.

Again, pride is a *brainless thing*, as well as a groundless thing, for it brings no profit with it. There is no wisdom in a self-exaltation. Other vices have some excuse, for men seem to gain by them—avarice, pleasure, lust have some plea—but the man who is proud sells his soul cheaply. He opens wide the floodgates of his heart to let men see how deep is the flood within his soul. Then suddenly it flows out, and all is gone—all is nothing for one puff of empty wind, one word of sweet applause. The soul is gone, and not a drop is left.

In almost every other sin, we gather up the ashes when the fire is gone. But here, what is left? The covetous man has his shining gold, but what does the proud man have? He has less than he would have had without his pride, and is no gainer whatever. Pride wins no crown. Men never honor it, not even the menial slaves of earth. All men look down on the proud man and think him less than themselves.

Again, pride is the *maddest thing* that can exist. It feeds upon its own vitals. It will take away its own life, that with its blood it may make a purple cape for its shoulders. It saps and undermines its own house that it may build its pinnacles a little higher, and then the whole structure tumbles down. Nothing proves men so mad as pride.

Then pride is a *protean thing* because changes its shape. It is all forms in the world. You may find it in any fashion you may choose. You may see it in the beggar's rags as well as in the rich man's garments. It dwells with the rich and with the poor. The man without a shoe to his foot may be as proud as if he were riding in a chariot.

Pride can be found in every rank of society, among all classes of men. Sometimes it is an Armenian and talks about the power of the creature. Then it turns Calvinist and boasts of its fancied security, forgetful of the Maker, who alone can keep our faith alive. Pride can profess any form of religion. It may be a Quaker and wear no collar to its coat. It may be a Episcopalian and worship God in splendid cathedrals. It may be a Dissenter and go to the common meeting house. It is one of the most catholic things in the world; it attends all kinds of chapels and churches. Go where you will, you will see pride. It comes up with us to the house of God. It goes with us to our houses. It is found in the market and the exchange, in the streets, and everywhere.

Let me hint at one or two forms which pride assumes. Sometimes pride takes the doctrinal shape. It teaches the doctrine of self-sufficiency. It tells us what man can do and will not admit that we are lost, fallen, debased, and ruined creatures, as we are. It hates divine sovereignty and rails at election.

Then, if pride is driven from that, it takes another form. It allows that the doctrine of free grace is true, but does not feel it. It acknowledges that salvation is of the Lord alone, but still it prompts men to seek heaven by their own works, even by the deeds of the law. When driven from that heresy, it will persuade men to join something with Christ in the matter of salvation.

When that is all torn up and the poor rag of our righteousness is all burned, pride will get into the Christian's heart as well as the sinner's. It will flourish under the name of self-sufficiency, teaching Christians that they are *"rich, have become wealthy, and have need of nothing"* (Revelation 3:17). It will tell them that they do not need daily grace, that past experience will do for tomorrow—that they know enough, toil enough, pray enough. It will make them forget that they have *"not...already attained"* (Philippians 3:12). It will not

8

allow them to press forward to the things that are ahead, forgetting the things that are behind. (See Philippians 3:13-14.) It enters into hearts and tempts believers to set up independent businesses for themselves. Until the Lord brings about a spiritual bankruptcy, pride will keep them from going to God.

Pride has ten thousand shapes. It is not always that stiff and starched gentleman that you picture. It is a vile, creeping, insinuating thing, that will twist itself like a serpent into our hearts. It will talk of humility and prate about being dust and ashes. I have known men to talk about their corruption most marvelously, pretending to be all humility, while at the same time they were the proudest wretches that could be found this side of the gulf of separation.

O friends! You cannot tell how many shapes pride will assume. Look sharp about you, or you will be deceived by it. And just when you think you are entertaining angels, you will find you have been receiving devils unawares.

The true throne of pride everywhere is the heart of man. If we desire, by God's grace, to put down pride, the only way is to begin with the heart.

Now let me tell you a parable in the form of an eastern story, which will set this truth in its proper light. A wise man in the East, called a dervish, in his wanderings came suddenly upon a mountain. He saw beneath his feet a smiling valley, in the midst of which there flowed a river. With the sun shining on the stream, the water, as it reflected the sunlight, looked pure and beautiful. When he descended, he found it was muddy, and the water utterly unfit for drinking.

Nearby he saw a young man, in the dress of a shepherd, who was filtering the water for his flocks with much diligence. One moment he poured some water into a pitcher and then allowed it to stand. After it had settled, he poured the clean fluid into a cistern. Then, in another place, he would be seen turning aside the current for a little, and letting it ripple over the sand and stones so that it might be filtered and the impurities removed.

The dervish watched the young man endeavoring to fill a large cistern with clear water. He asked him, "My son, why all this toil? What purpose does it answer?"

The young man replied, "Father, I am a shepherd. This water is so filthy that my flock will not drink it. Therefore, I am obliged to purify it little by little, so I collect enough in this way that they may drink, but it is hard work." So saying, he wiped the sweat from his brow, for he was exhausted with his toil.

"Right well have you labored," said the wise man, "but do you know your toil is not well applied? With half the labor, you might attain a better end. I envisage that the source of this stream must be impure and polluted. Let us take a pilgrimage together and see." They then walked some miles, climbing their way over many a rock, until they came to a spot where the stream took its rise. When they came near it, they saw flocks of wild fowls flying away, and wild beasts of the earth rushing into the forest. These had come to drink and had soiled the water with their feet. They found an open well which kept continually flowing, but, by reason of these creatures which perpetually disturbed it, the stream was always turbid and muddy.

"My son," said the wise man, "set to work now to protect the fountain and guard the well, which is the source of this stream. When you have done that, if you can keep these wild beasts and fowls away, the stream will flow by itself all pure and clear, and you will have no longer need for your toil." The young man did it, and as he labored, the wise man said to him, "My son, hear the word of wisdom. If you are wrong, seek not to correct your outward life, but seek first to get your heart correct, for out of it are the issues of life. Your life shall be pure when once your heart is so."

So if we would get rid of pride, we should not proceed to arrange our dress by adopting some special costume, or to qualify our language by using an outlandish tongue. Rather, let us seek of God that He would purify our hearts from pride. Then assuredly, if pride is purged from the heart, our life also shall be humble. Make the tree good, and then the fruit shall be good. Make the fountain pure, and the stream shall be sweet.

2

Good Works and Broken Keys

Faith is necessary to salvation, because we are told in Scripture that *works cannot save.* I want to tell a very familiar story, so even the poorest may not misunderstand what I say: A minister was one day going to preach. He climbed a hill on his road. Beneath him lay the villages, sleeping in their beauty, with the cornfields motionless in the sunshine. But he did not look at them, for his attention was arrested by a woman standing at her door. Upon seeing him, she came up with the greatest anxiety and said, "O sir, have you any keys about you? I have broken the key of my drawers, and there are some things that I must get directly."

He replied, "I have no keys." She was disappointed, expecting that everyone would have some keys. "But suppose," he said, "I had some keys, they might not fit your lock, and therefore you could not get the articles you want. But do not distress yourself. Wait till someone else comes up. But," said he wishing to improve the occasion, "have you ever heard of the key of heaven?"

"Ah, yes!" she said, "I have lived long enough and have gone to church long enough to know that if we work hard, get our bread by the sweat of our brow, act well towards our neighbors, behave 'lowly and reverently to all our betters' as the catechism says, and if we do our duty in that station of life in which it has pleased God to place us, and say our prayers regularly, we shall be saved."

"Ah!" said he, "My good woman, that is a broken key, for you have broken the commandments. You have not fulfilled all your duties. It is a good key, but you have broken it."

"Pray, sir," said she, believing that he understood the matter, and looking frightened, "what have I left out?"

"Why", said he, "the all-important thing—the blood of Jesus Christ. Don't you know it is said that the key of heaven is at His girdle. He opens, and no man shuts;

He shuts, and no man opens?" Explaining it more fully to her, he said, "It is Christ, and Christ alone, that can open heaven to you and not your good works."

"What, minister!" said she, "Are our good works useless, then?"

"No," said he, "not after faith. If you believe first, you may have as many good works as you please. But if you believe, you will never trust in them, for if you trust in them, you have spoiled them, and they are not good works any longer. Have as many good works as you please, but still put your trust wholly in the Lord Jesus Christ. If you do not, your key will never unlock heaven's gate."

So then we must have true faith, because the old key of works is so broken by us all that we never shall enter paradise by it. If you pretend that you have no sins, to be very plain with you, you deceive yourselves, and the truth is not in you. If you conceive that by your good works you shall enter heaven (never was there a more deadly delusion), you shall find at the last great day that your hopes were worthless, and that, like dry leaves from the autumn trees, your noblest doings shall be blown away or kindled into a flame in which you yourselves must suffer forever. Take heed of your good works. Do them after faith. Just remember, the way to be saved is simply to believe in Jesus Christ.

Without faith it is impossible to be saved and to please God, because without faith there is no *union to Christ*. Now, union to Christ is indispensable to our salvation. If I come before God's throne with my prayers, I shall never get them answered unless I bring Christ with me.

The Molossians of old, when they could not get a favor from their king, adopted a singular expedient. They took the king's only son in their arms and, falling on their knees, cried, "O king, for your son's sake, grant our request."

He smiled and said, "I deny nothing to those who plead in my son's name." It is so with God. He will deny nothing to the man who comes, having Christ at his elbow; but if he comes alone, he must be cast away. Union to Christ is, after all, the great point in salvation.

Let me tell you a story to illustrate this: The stupendous falls of Niagara have been spoken of in every part of the world. But while they are marvelous to hear of, and wonderful as a spectacle, they have been very destructive to human life when by accident any have been carried down the cataract. Some years ago, two men—a barge man and a collier—were in a boat and found themselves unable to manage it. It was being carried so swiftly down the current that they must both inevitably be borne down and dashed to pieces. Persons on the shore saw them but were unable to do much for their rescue. At last, however, one man was saved by floating a rope to him, which he grasped. The same instant that the rope came into his hand, a log floated by the other man. The thoughtless and confused barge man, instead of seizing the rope, laid hold of the log. It was a fatal mistake. They were both in imminent peril, but the one was drawn to shore because he had a connection with the people on the land, while the other, clinging to the log, was borne irresistibly along, never to be heard of afterwards.

Do you not see that here is a practical illustration? Faith is a connection with Christ. Christ is on the shore, so to speak, holding the rope of faith. If we lay hold of it with the hand of our confidence, He pulls us to shore. However, our good works, having no connection with Christ, are drifted along down the gulf of mortal despair. Grapple them as tightly as we may, even with hooks of steel, they cannot avail us in the least degree.

3

The Double-minded Man

Balaam said, *"I have sinned"* (Numbers 22:34), but yet he went on with his sin afterwards. One of the strangest characters of the whole world is Balaam. I have often marvelled at that man. He seems really in another sense to have come up to these lines by Ralph Erskine:

> To good and evil equal bent,
> And both a devil and a saint.

Balaam did seem to be so. At times no man could speak more eloquently and more truthfully, and at other times he exhibited the most mean and sordid covetousness that could disgrace human nature.

Imagine you see Balaam: he stands upon the brow of the hill. The multitudes of Israel lie at his feet. He is bidden to curse them, and he cries, *"How shall I curse whom God has not cursed?"* (Numbers 23:8).

As God opens his eyes, he even begins to tell about the coming of Christ by saying, *"I see Him, but not now: I behold Him, but not near"* (Numbers 24:17). He winds up his oration by saying, *"Let me die the death of the righteous, and let my end be like his!"* (Numbers 23:10). At this point you would say of that man that he is a hopeful character.

But wait until Balaam has come off the brow of the hill. Then you will hear him give the most diabolical advice to the king of Moab which it was even possible for Satan himself to suggest. Said he to the king, "You cannot overthrow these people in battle, for God is with them. Try to entice them from their God instead." (See Numbers 31:16.) And you know how the Moabites tried to entice the children of Israel from allegiance to Jehovah with wanton lusts.

Thus this man seemed to have the voice of an angel at one time, and yet the very soul of a devil in his bowels. He was a terrible character. He was a man of two things, a man who went all the way with two things to a very great extent. I know the Scripture says, *"No man can serve two masters"* (Matthew 6:24). Now this is often misunderstood. Some read it, *"No man can serve two."* Yes, he can—he can serve three or four. The way to read it is this, *"No man can serve two **masters**."* They cannot both be masters. He can serve two, but they cannot both be his master. A man can serve two who are not his masters, or even twenty. He may live for twenty different purposes, but he cannot live for more than one master purpose. There can only be one master purpose in his soul.

However, Balaam labored to serve two. It was like the people of whom it was said, *"They feared the LORD, yet served their own gods."* (2 Kings 17:33). Or like Rufus, who was cut from the same cloth. You know our old king Rufus painted God on one side of his shield and the devil on the other, and had underneath the motto: "Ready for both; catch who can."

There are many such people who are ready for both. They meet a minister, and how pious and holy they are! On the Sabbath, you would think they are the most respectable and upright people in the world. Indeed, they affect a drawling in their speech which they presume to be eminently religious. But on a week day, if you want to find the greatest rogues and cheats, they are some of those men who are so sanctimonious in their piety.

Now, rest assured that no confession of sin can be genuine unless it is a whole-hearted one. It is of no use for you to say, *"I have sinned,"* and then keep on sinning. *"I have sinned,"* say you, and it is a fair, fair face you show. But, alas, for the sin you will go away and commit!

Some men seem to be born with two characters. I remarked when in the library at Trinity College, Cambridge, about a very fine statue of Lord Byron. The librarian said to me, "Stand here, sir." I looked and said, "What a fine intellectual countenance! What a grand genius he was!" "Come here," the librarian said, "to the other side." "Ah, what a demon! There stands the man that could defy the Deity." He seemed to have such a scowl and such a dreadful leer in his face, even as Milton would have painted Satan when he said, "Better to reign in hell than serve in heaven." I turned away and asked the librarian, "Do you think the artist designed this?" "Yes," he said, "he wished to picture the two characters—the great, the grand, the almost superhuman genius that he possessed, and yet the enormous mass of sin that was in his soul."

There are some men of the same sort. I dare say, like Balaam, they would overthrow everything in argument with their enchantments. They could work miracles, and yet at the same time there is something about them which betrays a horrid character of sin, as great as that which would appear to be their character for righteousness. Balaam, you know, offered sacrifices to God upon the altar of Baal. That was just his character type. So many do the same. They offer sacrifices to God on the shrine of Mammon; while they will give to the building of a church and distribute to the poor, they will at the other door of the counting house grind the poor for bread and press the very blood out of the widow, that they may enrich themselves.

Ah! It is idle and useless for you to say, *"I have sinned,"* unless you mean it from your heart. That double-minded man's confession is of no avail.

4

A Drama In Five Acts
Based on 1 Corinthians 7:29-31

The first act introduces those that have wives. It opens with a wedding. The bride and bridegroom advance to the altar in bridal attire. The bells are ringing; crowds are cheering at the door, while overflowing mirth is supreme within. In another scene we observe domestic happiness and prosperity, a loving husband and a happy wife. Further on in the performance, rosy children are climbing the father's knee. The little prattles are lisping their mother's name.

"Now," says our theater companion as he gazes with rapture, "This is real and enduring, I know it is. This will satisfy me. I crave for nothing more than this. Home is a word as sweet as heaven, and a healthy, happy race of children is as fine a possession as even angels can desire. On this rock will I build all my hope. Secure me this portion, and I cheerfully renounce the dreamy joys of religion." We whisper in his ear that all this is but a changing scene which will by-and-by pass away, that time is short, and that his wife and children are dying creatures.

The man laughs at us and says, "Fanatics and enthusiasts may seek eternal joys, but these are enough for me." He believes that if there is anything permanent in the universe, it is marrying and being given in marriage, educating and bringing up a family, and seeing them all comfortably settled. He is right in valuing the blessing, but wrong in making it his all. Will he see his error before the curtain falls, or will he continue to base the hopes of an immortal spirit upon dying joys?

See the green mounds in the cemetery and the headstones inscribed "Here he lies." Alas for you, poor deluded worldling, where is your soul now? Does it console you that the dust of your offspring will mingle with your ashes? Where have you a home now? What family have you now to care for? The first act is over. Take a breath and say, *"This also is vanity."*

The tenor of the drama changes. Alas, how soon! Household joys are linked with household sorrows. They that weep are now before us in the second act. The cloudy and dark days have come. There are parents wringing their hands. A beloved child has died, and they are following its corpse to the tomb. Anon, the merchant has suffered a tremendous loss. He puts his hand to his aching head and mourns, for he knows not what will be the end of his troubles. The wife smitten by the hand of death lies on her bed, blanched with sickness and wan with pain. At her side is a weeping husband, and then there is another funeral. In the dim distance, I see the black horses again and again. The woes of men are frequent. Sorrow's visits are not, like those of angels, few and far between.

Our man of the world, who is much moved at this second act, foreseeing his own sorrows therein, weeps, until he fairly sobs out his feelings, clutches us with earnestness and cries, "Surely this is awfully real. You cannot call this a fleeting sorrow or a light affliction. I will wring my hands forever. The delight of my eyes has been taken from me. I have lost all my joys now. My beloved in whom I trusted has withered like a leaf in autumn before my face. Now shall I despair. I shall never look up again!"

"I have lost my fortune," says the afflicted merchant, "and distress overwhelms me. This world is indeed a wilderness to me. All its flowers are withered. I would not give a snap of my finger to live now, for everything worth living for is gone!"

Sympathizing deeply with our friend, we nevertheless venture to tell him that these trials to the Christian, because they are so short and produce such lasting good, are not killing sorrows. "Ah!" says he, "you men of faith may talk in that way, but I cannot. I tell you these are real things."

Like an English sailor, who, when seeing a play, leaped on the stage to help a lady in distress because he believed that the whole scene was real, so do such men weep and sigh as if they were to mourn forever because some earthly good has been removed. Oh, if they only knew that the depths of sorrow were never yet explored by a mortal mourner! Oh, that they would escape from those lower depths where immortal spirits weep and wail amid an emphasis of misery! The sorrows of time are trifles indeed when compared with the pains of everlasting punishment. On the other hand we reckon that they *are not worthy to be compared with the glory which shall be revealed in us*" (Romans 8:18). They are but light afflictions, which are but for a moment, a mere pin prick to the man of faith.

Happy is the man whose eyes are open to see that heirs of heaven do not sorrow as those who are without hope. A real joy of heavenly origin is ever with believers, and it is but the shadow of sorrow which falls upon them. There let the curtain drop, let us enter into an eternal state, and what and where are these temporary griefs?

The third act comes on and presents us with a view of those who rejoice. It may be that the first-born son has come of age, and there are great festivities. They are eating and drinking in the servants' hall and in the master's banquet chamber. There are high notes of joy and many compliments, and the smiling sire is as glad as a man can be. Or it is the daughter's wedding where kind friends implore a thousand blessings on her head, and the father smiles and shares the joy. Or it is a gain in business, a fortunate speculation, or the profits of industry have come flowing in, slowly perhaps, but still surely. The man is full of rejoicing: he has a house, home, friends, reputation, and honor. He is, in the eyes of all who know him, happy. Those who do not know him think that he has no cares, that he can have no sorrows, that his life must be one perpetual feast, and that, surely there can be no spot in his sun, no winter in his year, no ebb to follow his floods.

Our friend by our side is smiling at this sunny picture. "There," says he, "is not that real? Why, there must be something in that! What more do you want? Only let me get the same, and I will leave you the joys of faith, and heaven, and immortality to yourselves. These are the things for me. Only let me laugh and make merry, and you may pray as you will. Fill high the bowl for me. Put the roast and food on the table, and let me eat and drink, for tomorrow I die."

If we gently hint to our friend that all this passes away like a vision of the night, and that we have learned to look on it as though it did not exist, he laughs us to scorn, and accounts us mad when he is most mad himself. As for ourselves, far from resting upon the softest couch that earth can give us, we instead spurn its vain delights.

But the fourth act of the drama is before us. They that buy demand our attention. The merchant is neither a man of mirth nor a mourner. In the eyes of certain Mammonites he is attending to the one sure necessity, the most substantial of all concerns. Here feast your eyes, you hard, practical, earth-dwellers. There are his money bags. Hear how they thump on the table! There are the rolls of bonds, the banker's books, the title deeds of estates, mortgages and securities, and the solid investment in his government's own treasury notes. He has made a good thing of life, and still he adheres to business, as he should do. Like any painstaking man, he is accumulating still and piling up his heap, meanwhile adding field to field and estate to estate, until soon he will possess a whole country. He has just now been buying a large and very fine house, where he intends to spend the remainder of his days, for he is about to retire from business. The lawyer is busy making out the transfer, the sum of money is waiting to be paid, and the whole thing is as good as settled.

"Ah, now," says our friend, who is looking on at the play, "you are not going to tell me that this is all a shadow! It is not. There is something very solid and real here, at least, something that will perfectly satisfy me." We tell him we dare say there is something that will satisfy him, but our desires are of a larger span, and nothing but the Infinite can fill them.

Alas for the man who can find satisfaction in earthly things! It will be only for a time. When he comes to lie upon his death bed, he will find his buying and his selling are poor things with which to stuff a dying pillow. He will find that his gaining and his acquisitions bring but little comfort to an aching heart, and no peace to a conscience exercised with the fear of the wrath to come. "Ah, ah!" he cries, and sneers sarcastically, putting us aside as only fit for Bedlam, "Let me trade and make a fortune, and that is enough for me. With that I shall be well content!" Alas, poor fool, the snow melts not sooner than the joy of wealth, and the smoke of the chimney is as solid as the comfort of riches!

But we must not miss the fifth act. See the rich man, our friend whom lately we saw married, whom we saw in trouble,

31

afterwards rejoicing and prospering in business. He has entered upon a ripe old age. He has retired and has now come to use the world. The world says he has been a wise man and has done well, for all men will praise you when you do well for yourself. Now he keeps a liberal table, a fine garden, excellent horses, and many servants. He has all the comforts in fact that wealth can command.

As you look around his noble park, as you gaze at his avenue of fine old trees, or stay a day or two at the family mansion and notice all its luxuries, you hear your friend saying, "Aye, there is something very real here. What do you think of this?"

We hint that the grey hairs of the owner of all these riches foreshadow that his time is short, and that if this is all he has, he is a very poor man. He will soon have to leave it, and his regrets in leaving will make his death more pitiable than that of a pauper. Our friend replies, "Ah! You are always talking in this way. I tell you this is not a play. I believe it is all real and substantial, and I am not, by any talking of yours, to be made to think that it is unsubstantial and will soon be gone."

O world, you have fine actors, to cheat men so well, or else mortal man is an easy fool, taken in your net like the fishes of the sea. The whole matter is most palpably a show, but yet men give their souls to win it. *"Why do you spend money for what is not bread, and your wages for what does not satisfy?"* (Isaiah 55:2).

5

The Table of the Profligate

The Banquet of Evil

Take a warning glance at the house of feasting which Satan has built. Just as wisdom has built her house and hewn out her seven pillars, so has folly its temple and its tavern of feasting into which it continually tempts the unwary. Look within the banqueting house, and I will show you four tables and the guests that sit there. As you look at those tables, you will see the courses brought in.

At the first table to which I shall invite your attention, though I beseech you never to sit down there and partake, sit the profligates. The table of the profligate is a gay table, covered over with a gaudy crimson. All the vessels upon it look exceedingly bright and glistening. Many there are that sit there, but they know not that they are the guests of hell and that the end of all the feasting shall be in the depths of perdition. See the great governor of the feast as he comes in? He has a bland smile upon his face. His garments are not black, but he is girded with a robe of many colors. He has a honeyed word on his lip and a tempting witchery in the sparkle of his eye. He brings in the cup and says, "Hey, young man, drink here. It sparkles in the cup. It moves well. Do you see it? It is the wine cup of pleasure." This is the first cup at the banqueting house of Satan. The young man takes it and sips the liquor. At first it is a cautious sip. It is but a little he will take, and then he will restrain himself.

He does not intend to indulge much in lust; he means not to plunge headlong into perdition. There is a flower there on the edge of that cliff. He will reach forward a little and pluck it, but it is not his intention to dash himself from that jutting crag and destroy himself. Not he! He thinks it easy to put away the cup when he has tested its flavor! He has no design to abandon himself to its intoxication.

He takes a shallow sip. But how sweet it is! How it makes his blood tingle within him! What a fool I was not to have tasted this before! he thinks. Was ever joy like this? Could it be thought that bodies could be capable of such ecstasy as this? He drinks again. This time he takes a deeper draught, and the wine is hot in his veins. Oh, how blessed is he! What would he not say now in praise of Bacchus, or Venus, or whatever other shape Beelzebub chooses to assume? He becomes a very orator in praise of sin! It is fair. It is pleasant. The deep damnation of lust appears as joyous as the transports of heaven. He drinks, he drinks, he drinks again, until his brain begins to reel with the intoxication of his sinful delight.

This is the first course. Drink, you drunkards of Ephraim, and bind the crown of pride about your head, and call us fools because we put your cup from us. Drink with the harlot, and dine with the lustful. You may think yourselves wise for so doing, but we know that after these things there comes something worse. Your vine is the vine of Sodom and of the fields of Gomorrah. Your grapes are grapes of gall, the clusters are bitter. Your wine is the poison of dragons and the cruel venom of asps.

Now, with a leer upon his brow, the subtle governor of the feast rises from his seat. His victim has had enough of the best wine. He takes away that cup, and he brings in another, not quite so sparkling. Look into the liquor. It is not beaded over with the sparkling bubbles of rapture. It is all flat, dull, and insipid. It is called the cup of satiety. The man has had enough of pleasure. Like a dog he vomits, though like a dog he will return to his vomit yet again. Who has woe? Who has redness of eyes? They that tarry long at the wine. I am now speaking figuratively of wine, as well as literally. The wine of lust brings the same redness of the eyes.

The profligate soon discovers that all the rounds of pleasure end in satiety. "What," says he, "what more can I do? There, I have committed every wickedness that can be imagined, and I have drained every cup of pleasure. Give me something fresh! I have gone to every kind of pleasure that I can conceive. There, I don't care so much as one single farthing for them all. It is all over. Gaiety itself grows flat and dull. What am I to do?"

This is the devil's second course—the course of satiety—a fitful drowsiness, the result of the previous excess. Thousands there are who are drinking of the tasteless cup of satiety every day. Some novel invention by which they may kill time, some new discovery whereby they may give a fresh vent to their iniquity, would be a wonderful thing to them. If some man should rise up who could find out for them some new fashion of wickedness, some deeper depths in the deeps of the bottom-most hell of lasciviousness, they would bless his name for having given them something fresh to excite them.

That is the devil's second course. And do you see them partaking of it? There are some of you that are having a deep draught of it. You are the jaded horses of the fiend of lust, the disappointed followers of the will-o'-the-wisp of pleasure. God knows, if you were to speak your heart out, you would be obliged to say, "There! I have tried pleasure, and I do not find it pleasure. I have gone all around, and I am just like the blind horse at the mill. I have to go round again. I am spellbound to the sin, but I cannot take delight in it now as I once did, for all the glory of it is as a fading flower and as the hasty fruit before the summer."

For awhile the feaster remains in the putrid sea of his infatuation, but another scene is opening. The governor of the feast commands another liquor to be broached. This time the fiend bears a black goblet, and he presents it with eyes full of hell-fire, flashing with fierce damnation. "Drink of that, sir," says he. The man sips it, starts back, and shrieks, "O God, that ever I must come to this!" But he must drink, for he that quaffs the first cup must drink the second and the third.

Drink, though it be like fire down your throat! Drink it, though it be as the lava of Etna in your bowels! Drink! You must drink! He that sins must suffer. He that is a profligate in his youth must have rotten-ness in his bones and disease within his loins. He who rebels against the laws of God must reap the harvest in his own body here.

Oh, there are some dreadful things that I might tell you of this third course. Satan's house has a front hall full of every-thing that is enticing to the eye and be-witching to the sensual taste. But there is a back chamber, and no one knows, no one has seen the whole of its horrors. There is a secret chamber where he shovels out the creatures whom he has himself destroyed —a chamber beneath whose floor is the blazing of hell, and above whose boards the heat of that horrible pit is felt.

It may be a physician's place, rather than mine, to tell of the horrors that some suffer as the result of their iniquity. I leave that to them. But let me tell the profligate spendthrift that the poverty he will endure is the result of his sin of extravagant waste. Let him know also that the remorse of conscience that will overtake him is not an accidental thing that drops by chance from heaven. It is rather the result of his own iniquity. You may depend upon it, men and brethren, sin carries an infant misery in its bowels, and sooner or later it must be delivered of its terrible child. If we sow the seed, we must reap the harvest. Thus the law of hell's house stands: first, the good wine, then afterwards, that which is worse.

The last course remains to be presented. Now, strong men, who mock at the warning which I would rather deliver to you with a brother's voice and with an affectionate heart though with rough language, come here and drink of this last cup. The sinner has at the end brought himself to the grave. His hopes and joys were put into a bag full of holes, and they have all vanished—vanished forever. Now he has come to the end. His sins haunt him. His transgressions perplex him. He is taken like a bull in a net, and how shall he escape? He dies and descends from disease to damnation. Shall mortal language attempt to tell you the horrors of that last tremendous cup of which the profligate must drink and drink forever? Look at it. You cannot see its depths, but cast an eye upon its seething surface.

I hear the noise of rushing frantically, and a sound of gnashing of teeth and the wailing of despairing souls. I look into that cup and hear a voice coming up from its depths, *"These shall go away into everlasting punishment"* (Matthew 25:46), *"for Tophet was established of old...its pyre is fire with much wood; the breath of the LORD, like a stream of brimstone, kindles it"* (Isaiah 30:33).

And what do you say to this last course of Satan? *"Who among us shall dwell with the devouring fire?"* (Isaiah 33:14). Profligate, I beseech you, in the name of God, leave this table! Oh, be not so careless at your cups. Be not so asleep, secure in the peace which you now enjoy! Death is at the door, and at his heels is swift destruction! As for you, who have been restrained until now by a careful father and the watchfulness of an anxious mother, I urge you to shun the house of sin and folly. Let the wise man's words be written on your heart, and be mindful of them in the hour of temptation. *"Remove your way far from her, and do not go near the door of her house...For the lips of am immoral woman drip honey, and her mouth is smoother than oil; but in the end she is bitter as wormwood, sharp as a two-edged sword. Her feet go down to death; her steps lay hold of hell"* (Proverbs 5:8, 3-4).

6

The Self-Righteous Guests

The Banquet of Evil

Do you see that table over yonder, in the middle of the palace? Ah, good easy souls! Many of you had thought that you never went to the feast of hell at all, but there is a table for you, too. It is covered over with a fair white cloth, and all the vessels upon the table are very clean and comely. The wine looks not like the wine of Gomorrah. It flows smoothly, like the wine from the grapes of Eshcol. It seems to have no intoxication in it. It is like the ancient wine which they pressed from the grape into the cup, having in it no deadly poison.

Do you see the men who sit at this table? How self-contented they are! Ask the white fiends who wait about it, and they will tell you, "This is the table of the self-righteous. The Pharisee sits here. You may know him. He has his phylactery between his eyes. The hem of his garment is made exceedingly broad. He is one of the best of the best professors."

"Ah!" says Satan, as he draws the curtain and shuts off the table where the profligates are carousing, "Be quiet. Don't make so much noise, lest these sanctimonious hypocrites guess what company they are in. These self-righteous people are my guests quite as much as you, and I have them quite as safely."

So Satan, like an angel of light, brings forth a gilded goblet, looking like the chalice of the table of communion. What wine is that? It seems to be the very wine of the sacred Eucharist. However, it is called the wine of self-satisfaction, and around the brim you may see the bubbles of pride. Look at the swelling froth upon the bowl. *"God, I thank You that I am not like other men; extortioners, unjust, adulterers, or even as this tax collector"* (Luke 18:11). You know that cup, my self-deceiving readers. Oh, if only you knew the deadly hemlock which is mixed in there! Sin as other men do? Not you! Not at all! You are not going to submit yourself to the righteousness of Christ. Why should you? You are as good as your neighbors. If you are not saved, you ought to be, you think. After all, don't you pay everybody a full twenty shillings to the pound? Did you ever rob anybody in your life? You do your neighbors a good turn. You are as good as other people.

That is the first cup the devil gives. The good wine makes you swell with self-important dignity, as its fumes enter your heart and puff it up with an accursed pride. Yes, I see you sitting in the room so cleanly swept and so neatly garnished. I see the crowds of your admirers standing around the table, even many of God's own children, who say, "Oh, that I were half as good as he!" The very humility of the righteous provides you with fuel for your pride.

Wait awhile, you unctuous hypocrite. Wait awhile, for there is a second course to come. Satan looks upon these guests with quite the same self-satisfied air as he did upon the troop of rioters. "Ah!" says he, "I cheated those gay fellows with the cup of pleasure. I gave them afterwards the dull cup of satiety, and I have cheated you, too. You think yourselves all right, but I have deceived you twice. I have fooled you indeed." So he brings in a cup which he himself does not like to serve sometimes. It is called the cup of discontentment and mental disquiet. Many there are that have to drink this after all their self-satisfaction. Do you not find, you who are very good in your own esteem but have no interest in Christ, that when you sit alone and begin to turn over your accounts for eternity, they do not square somehow? You cannot seem to strike the balance exactly to your own side after all, as you thought you could. Have you not sometimes found, when you thought you were standing on a rock, there was a quivering beneath your feet?

You heard the Christian sing boldly:

"Bold shall I stand in that great day,
For who aught to my charge shall lay?
While through your blood absolved I am
From sin's tremendous curse and shame."

You have replied, "Well, I cannot sing that. I have been as good a churchman as ever lived. I never missed going to my church all these years, but I cannot say I have a solid confidence." You once had a hope of self-satisfaction, but now the second course has been served, and you are not quite so contented.

"Well," says another, "I have been to my chapel, and I have been baptized, and made a profession of religion, though I was never brought to know the Lord in sincerity and in truth. I once thought it was all well with me, but I want something which I cannot find." Now comes a shaking in the heart. It is not quite as delightful as it was supposed to be building on one's own righteousness. Ah, that is the second course.

Wait awhile, and, perhaps in this world but certainly in the hour of death, the devil will bring in the third cup of dismay at the discovery of your lost condition. How many a man who has been self-righteousness all his life has, at the last, discovered that the thing on which he placed his hope had failed him!

I have heard of an army who, being defeated in battle, endeavored to make a good retreat. With all their might, the soldiers fled to a certain river where they expected to find a bridge across which they could retreat and be in safety. But when they came to the stream, there was heard a shriek of terror, "The bridge is broken, the bridge is broken!" All in vain was that cry, for the multitude hurrying on behind pressed upon those that were before and forced them into the river, until the stream was glutted with the bodies of drowned men.

Such must be the fate of the self-righteous. You thought there was a bridge of ceremonies—that baptism, confirmation, and the Lord's Supper made up the solid arches of a bridge of good works and duties. But when you come to die, there shall be heard the cry, "The bridge is broken, the bridge is broken!"

It will be in vain for you to turn around then. Death is close behind you. He forces you onward, and you discover what it is to perish through having neglected the great salvation and attempting to save yourself through your own good works.

This is the last course except one. Your last course of all, the worst wine, your everlasting portion must be the same as that of the profligate. Good as you thought yourself to be, inasmuch as you proudly rejected Christ, you must drink the wine cup of the wrath of God, that cup which is full of trembling. The wicked of the earth shall wring out the dregs of that cup and drink them. You also must drink of it as deeply as they.

Oh, beware the time! Put away your high looks, and *"humble yourselves under the mighty hand of God"* (1 Peter 5:6). *"Believe on the Lord Jesus Christ, and you will be saved"* (Acts 16:31).

7

The Worldly-Wise

The Banquet of Evil

You have, as yet, escaped the lash. However, a third table is crowded with most honorable guests. I believe there have been more princes and kings, mayors and aldermen, and great merchants sitting at this table than at any other. It is called the table of worldliness.

"Humph!" says a man, "I dislike the profligate. There's my eldest son. I've been hard at work saving up money all my life, but that young fellow will not stick to business. He has become a real profligate. I am very glad the minister spoke so sharp about that.

"As for me, there now! I don't care about your self-righteous people a single farthing. To me it is of no account at all. I don't care at all about religion in the slightest degree. I like to know whether the funds rise or fall, or whether there is an opportunity of making a good bargain, but that's about all I care for."

Ah, worldling! I have read of a friend of yours who was clothed in scarlet and fine linen, and who fared sumptuously every day. Do you know what became of him? You should remember it, for the same end awaits you. The end of his feast must be the end of yours. If your god is this world, depend upon it that you shall find your way is full of bitterness.

Now, see that table of the worldly man, the mere worldling who lives for gain. Satan brings him in a flowing cup, "There," says he, "young man, you are starting in business. You need not care about the conventionalities of honesty or about the ordinary, old-fashioned fancies of religion. Get rich as quickly as you can. Get money. Get money honestly if you can, but if not, get it anyhow," says the devil, and down he puts his tankard. "There," says he, "is a foaming draught for you." "Yes," says the young man, "I have abundance now. My hopes are indeed realized." Here, then, you see the first and best wine of the worldling's feast, and many of you are tempted to envy this man. "Oh, that I had such a prospect in business!" says one. "I am not half as sharp as he is. I could not deal as he deals. My religion would not let me. But how dare he get rich! Oh, that I could prosper as he does!"

Come, my brother, judge not before the time. There's a second course to come—the thick and nauseous draught of care. The man has obtained his money, but those who will be rich fall into temptation and a snare. Wealth, ill-gotten, ill-used, or hoarded, brings a canker with it that does not infect the gold and silver, but infects the man's heart. And a cankered heart is one of the most awful things a man can have. Ah! See this money-lover, and mark the care which sits upon his heart.

There is a poor old woman who lives near his lodge gate. She has but a pittance a week, but she says, "Bless the Lord, I have enough!" She never asks how she is to live, or how she is to die, or how she is to be buried, but sleeps sweetly on the pillow of contentment and faith. But here is this poor fool with untold gold, yet he is miserable because he happened to drop a six pence as he walked along the streets, or because he had an extra call upon his charity to which the presence of some friend compelled him to yield, or perhaps because his coat wears out too soon.

After this comes avarice. Many have to drink of that cup. May God save us from its fiery drops! A great American preacher has said:

> Covetousness breeds misery. The sight of houses better than our own, of dress beyond our means, of jewels costlier than we may wear, of stately equipage and rare curiosities beyond our reach—these hatch the viper brood of covetous thoughts, vexing the poor who would be rich, tormenting the rich who would be richer. The covetous man pines to see pleasure, is sad in the presence of cheerfulness, and the joy of the world is his sorrow because all the happiness of others is not his.
>
> I do not wonder that God abhors him. He inspects his heart as he would a cave full of noisy birds or a nest of rattling reptiles, and loathes the sight of its crawling tenants. To the covetous man life is a nightmare, and God lets him wrestle with it as best he may. Mammon might build its palace on such a heart, and pleasure might bring all its revelry there. Honor all its garlands—it would be like pleasures in a sepulchre, and garlands on a tomb.

When a man becomes avaricious, all he has is nothing to him. "More, more, more!" says he, like some poor creatures in a terrible fever who cry, "Drink, drink, drink!" You give them drink, but after they have it, their thirst increases. Like the horseleech, they cry, "Give, give, give!" (See Proverbs 30:15.) Avarice is a raving madness which seeks to grasp the world in its arms, and yet despises the plenty it has already.

This is a curse of which many have died. Some have died with the bag of gold in their hands and with misery upon their brow, because they could not take it with them into their coffin and could not carry it into another world.

Well, then, there comes the next course. Baxter and those terrible old preachers used to picture the miser and the man who lived only to acquire gold, sitting in the middle of hell with Mammon pouring melted gold down their throats. "There," say the mocking devils, "that is what you wanted. You have got it now. Drink, drink, drink!" as the molten gold is poured down.

I shall not, however, indulge in any such terrible imaginations. But this much

I know: he that lives to himself here must perish, and he who sets his affections upon things on earth has not dug deep but has built himself a house upon the sands. When the rain descends and the floods come, down must come his house, and great must be the fall of it. (See Matthew 7:26-27.)

It is the best wine first, however. It is for the respectable man—respectable and respected—whom everybody honors. Afterwards that which is worst is served, when meanness has sapped his wealth and covetousness has maddened his brain. It is sure to come, as sure as ever you give yourself up to worldliness.

The fourth table is set in a very secluded corner, in a very private part of Satan's palace. There is the table set for secret sinners, and here the old rule is observed. At that table, in a room well darkened, I see a young man sitting. Satan is the waiter, stepping in so noiselessly that no one would hear him. He brings in the first cup. How sweet it is! It is the cup of secret sin.

"Stolen waters are sweet, and bread eaten in secret is pleasant" (Proverbs 9:17). How sweet that morsel is when eaten all alone! Was there ever one that rolled so

delicately under the tongue? That is the first. After that Satan brings in another, the wine of an disturbed conscience. The man's eyes are opened. He says, "What have I done? What have I been doing?" cries this Achan, "In the first cup you brought me, I saw a wedge of gold and a goodly Babylonian garment sparkling. I thought, 'Oh, I must have that.' But now my thought is, 'What shall I do to hide this, where shall I put it? I must dig. Aye, I must dig deep as hell before I shall hide it, for sure enough it will be discovered.'"

The grim governor of the feast is bringing in a massive bowl filled with a black mixture. The secret sinner drinks and is confounded. He fears his sin will find him out. He has no peace, no happiness. He is full of uneasy fear. He is afraid that he shall be detected. He dreams at night that there is someone after him. There is a voice whispering in his ear and telling him, "I know all about it. I will tell it." He thinks, perhaps, that the sin which he has committed in secret will break out to his friends. His father will know it, and his mother will find out. Aye, it may be even the physician will tell the tale and blab out the wretched secret. He is always ill, dreading arrest.

For such a man there is no rest. He is like the debtor I have read of, who, owing a great deal of money, was afraid the bailiffs were after him. Happening one day to catch his sleeve on the top of a palisade, the debtor cried, "There, let me go. I'm in a hurry. I will pay you tomorrow," imagining that someone was laying hold of him. Such is the position in which the man places himself by partaking of the hidden things of dishonesty and sin.

Thus he finds no rest for the sole of his foot for fear of discovery. At last the discovery comes. It is the last cup. Often it comes on earth. *"Be sure your sin will find you out"* (Numbers 32:23), and it will generally find you out here. What frightful exhibitions are to be seen at our police courts of men who are made to drink that last black draught of discovery!

The man who presided at religious meetings, the man who was honored as a saint, is at last unmasked. And what do the judge and the world say of him? He is a jest, a reproach, and a rebuke everywhere.

But, suppose he should be so crafty that he lives his life without discovery —though I think it is almost impossible—

what a cup he must drink when he stands at last before the bar of God! "Bring him forth, jailor! Dread keeper of the dungeon of hell, lead forth the prisoner." He comes! The whole world is assembled. "Stand up, sir! Did you not make a profession of faith? Did not everybody think you were a saint?" He is speechless. But many there are in that vast crowd who cry, "We thought he was." The book is open; his deeds are read. Transgression after transgression are all laid bare. Do you hear that hiss? The righteous, moved to indignation, are lifting up their voices against the man who deceived them and dwelt among them as a wolf in sheep's clothing.

Oh, how fearful it must be to bear the scorn of the universe! The good can bear the scorn of the wicked, but for the wicked to bear the shame and everlasting contempt which righteous indignation will heap upon them will be one of the most frightful tortures. Of course, the worst is the eternal endurance of the wrath of the Most High, which, I need not add, is the last cup of the devil's terrible feast with which the secret sinner must be filled forever and ever.

8

Going through the Fire

I see iniquity raging on every side. Its flames are fanned by every wind of fashion. Fresh victims are being constantly drawn in. It spreads to every class. Not the palace nor the home is safe, not the lofty piles that are raised for merchandise, nor the graceful edifice that is constructed for worship. Iniquity, whose contagion is fearful as fire, spreads and preys upon all things that are homely and comely. Things useful and things sacred are not exempt. We must walk through the fire. We who are God's witnesses must stand in its very midst to pour the streams of living water upon the burning fuel. If we are not able to quench it, at least we must strive to prevent its spread.

I see in my mind's eye the blackened skeletons of hundreds of fair professions.

Multitudes—multitudes have perished in the valley of temptation, who once, to all human judgment, had a fair bid for heaven and made a show in the flesh. How many, too, have fallen under the attacks of Satan!

This is a fire that does burn. Many a man has said, "I will be a pilgrim," but he has met Apollyon on the road and has turned back. Many a man has put on the harness but has given up the battle too soon. He has put his hand to the plow and looked back. There are more pillars of salt than one. If Lot's wife were a solitary specimen, it would have been well. But there have been tens of thousands who, like her, have looked back to the plains of Sodom. Consequently, as they are in their spirits like her, they stand forever as what they were—lost souls.

We ought not to look upon our dangers with contempt. They are dangers, they are trials. We ought to look upon our temptations as fires. Oh, they are fires! If you think they are not fires, you are mistaken. If you enter, then, in your own strength, saying, "Oh, I could bear them," you will find that they are real fires which, with forked tongues, shall lick up your blood and consume it in an instant if you have not some better guard than your own native power.

"When you walk through the fire, you shall not be burned, neither shall the flame kindle upon you" (Isaiah 43:2 KJV). Dr. Alexander, an eminent and most admirable American commentator, says there appears to be some mistake in the translation, because he thinks the two sentences are an anti-climax. *"You shall not be burned,"* and then follows, *"neither shall the flame kindle upon you."* It strikes me, however, that in the second clause we have the higher gradation of a climax. *"You shall not be burned"* to the point of destruction of your life, nor even scorched to give you the most superficial injury, for *"the flames shall not kindle upon you."* Just as when the three holy children came out of the fiery furnace, it is said, *"Upon whose bodies the fire had no power; the hair of their head was not singed nor were their garments affected, and the smell of fire passed on them"* (Daniel 3:27).

Thus, the text seems to me to teach that the Christian church, under all its trials, has not been consumed, but more than that, it has not lost anything by its trials. The Lord's church has never been destroyed yet by her persecutors and her trials. They have thought they crushed her, but she lives still. They had imagined that they had taken away her life, but she sprang up more vigorous than before.

I suppose there is not a nation out of which Christ's church has ever been utterly driven. Even Spain, which seemed to have accomplished it by the most persevering barbarities, finds still a few believers to be a thorn in the side of her bigotry. As for our own denomination, in the very country where, by the most frightful massacres, it was believed that the sect of Anabaptists had been utterly extinguished, Mr. Oncken became the means of reviving it, so that throughout all Germany, and in parts of Denmark, Prussia, Poland, and even Russia itself, we have sprung up into a new, vigorous, and even wonderful existence. And in Sweden, where, under Lutheran government, the most persecuting edicts had been passed against us, we have been astonished to find churches suddenly spring up, for the truth has in it a living seed which is not to be destroyed.

But the church not only does not lose her existence, she does not lose anything at all. The church has never lost her numbers.

Persecutions have winnowed her and driven away the chaff, but not one grain of wheat has been taken away from the heap. No, not even in visible fellowship has the church been decreased by persecution. She is like Israel in Egypt: the more they were afflicted, the more they multiplied. Was a bishop put to death today? Ten young men came the next morning before the Roman proctor and offered themselves to die, having that very night been baptized for the dead bishop, having made their confession of faith that they might occupy his position. "I fill up the vacancy in the church and then die as he did." Was a woman strangled or tortured publicly? Twenty women appeared the next day and craved to suffer as she suffered, that they might honor Christ.

Did the Church of Rome in more modern times burn one of our glorious reformers, John Huss? Yet did not Martin Luther come forward as if the ashes of Huss had begotten Luther? When Wycliffe passed away, did not the very fact of Wycliffe being persecuted help to spread his doctrines? Were there not found hundreds of young men in every market town in England reading the Lollard's Scriptures and proclaiming the Lollard's faith? And so depend upon it, it shall ever be.

Give a dog a bad name, and you hang him; give a Christian a bad name, and you honor him. Do but give to any Christian some ill name, and before long a Christian denomination will take that name to itself, and it will become a title of honor. When George Fox was called "Quaker," it was a strange name—one to laugh at. But those men of God who followed him called themselves Quakers too, and so it lost its reproach. They called the followers of Whitefield and Wesley "Methodists." They took the title of Methodists, and it became a respectful designation.

When many of our Baptist forefathers, persecuted in England, went over to America to find shelter, they imagined that among the Puritans they would have a perfect rest. However, Puritan liberty of conscience meant, "The right and liberty to think as they did, but no toleration to those who differed." The Puritans of New England, as soon as a Baptist made his appearance among them, persecuted him with as little compunction as the Episcopalians had the Puritans. No sooner was there a Baptist, than he was hunted up and brought before his own Christian brethren. Mark you, he was brought up for fine, imprisonment, confiscation, and banishment before the very men who had themselves suffered persecution.

What was the effect of this? The effect has been that in America, where we were persecuted, we are the largest body of Christians. Where the fire burned the most furiously, there the good old Calvinistic doctrine was taught, and the Baptist became the more decidedly a Baptist than anywhere else, with the most purity and the least dross. Nor have we ever lost the firmness of our grip upon the fundamental doctrine for which our forefathers stained the baptismal pool with blood by all the trials and persecutions that have been laid upon us, and never shall we.

Upon the entire church, at the last, there shall not be even the smell of fire. I see her come out of the furnace. I see her advance up the hill towards her final glory with her Lord and Master. The angels look at her garments; they are not tattered. No, the fangs of her enemies have not been able to make a single tear therein. They draw near to her and look upon her flowing ringlets; they are not crisp with heat. They look upon her very feet; though she has trodden the coals, they are not blistered. Her eyes have not been dried up by the ferocity of the seven-times-heated flame. She has been made more beautiful, more fair, more glorious by the fires, but hurt she has not been, nor can she be.

Turn, then, to the individual Christian, and remember that the promise stands alike firm and fast with each believer. Christian, if you are truly a child of God, your trials cannot destroy you. Even better still, you can lose nothing by them. You may seem to lose for today, but when the account comes to be settled, you shall not be found to be a farthing the loser by all the temptations of all the world or all the attacks of Satan which you have endured. No, you shall be wondrously the gainer. Your trials, having worked patience and experience, shall make you rich. Your temptations, having taught you your weakness and shown you where your strength lies, shall make you strong.

There is a brother who has had wave upon wave of affliction. Everything goes against him. He is an upright, honest, indefatigable merchant, yet, let him do what he will, his substance wastes away like snow before the sun. It appears that, for every ship of his, the wind blows the wrong way, and where others win by the venture, he loses all.

> Sees every day new straits attend,
> And wonders where the scene shall end.

When I spoke of walking through the fire, he said, "Ah! That is what I have been doing. I have been walking through it these months. To God and my own soul alone is it known how hot the furnace is."

Brother, will you take home this text? *"When you walk through the fire, you shall not be burned."* When your troubles are all over, you shall still be left, and what is more, *"Neither shall the flame kindle upon you."* When the winding up time comes, you shall not be any the loser. While you think you have lost substance, you shall find when you read Scripture that you only lose shadows. Your substance was always safe, being laid up in the keeping of Christ in heaven. You shall discover in the issue, that these trials of yours were the best things that could happen to you. The day will come when you will say with David, *"I will sing of mercy and justice"* (Psalm

101:1). *"Before I was afflicted I went astray, but now I keep Your word"* (Psalm 119:67).

Perhaps there is some young woman in very bad straits. The case I am about to paint is a common one—alas, too common in this city. You love the Savior, my sister, but you are very poor, and you have to earn your living by that sorriest of all means. When the sun rises in the morning, He sees you with that needle in your hand, "Sewing at once with a double thread, a shroud as well as a shirt." All day long you have scarcely time to rest for meals. At evening time, when your fingers are worn and your eyes are heavy, you have need to refrain from sleep because the pittance is so small that you can scarcely live upon it. We know hundreds of that class who always constrain our pity, because they work so hard for such little wages.

Perhaps your mother is dead, and your father does not care about you. He is a drunken sot, and you would be sorry to meet him in the street. You have no helper, no friends. You do not care to tell anybody. You would not like to take anything if charity should offer it to you. You feel it is the hardest thing of all to be tempted as you are. There seems to be open to you the pathway to plenty and in some degree to delight. But you have said, "No, no!" You have loathed the temptation, and you have stood. I have known how year after year some of you have fought with temptation and struggled on, when sometimes you were close to starvation. But you would not do this great wickedness against God.

My sister, I pray you, take the encouragement of Scripture to strengthen you for the future battles. You have been going through the fires, but you are not consumed. I bless God, upon your garments the smell of fire has not passed. Hold on, my sister, through all the sorrow you have, and all the bitterness which is heavy enough to crush your spirit. Hold on, for your Master sees you. He will encourage and strengthen you, and bring you more than a conqueror through it all in the end.

How cruel sometimes worldly young men are to Christian young men! Cruel, for when there are a dozen worldlings and only one Christian, they consider it to be honorable for the dozen to set upon one. Twelve big, tall fellows will sometimes think it a fine game to pass from hand to hand some little lad of fifteen, making sport and mockery of him. There is honor, it is said, among thieves, but there seems to be no honor at all among worldlings when they get a young Christian in this way.

Young man, you have borne with it. You have said, "I will hold my tongue and won't say a word," though your heart was hot within you and the fire burned while you were musing. Remember, the anvil does not get broken, even if you keep on striking it, but it breaks all the hammers. You do the same. Hold on, and these fires shall not consume you. If the fire should burn up your piety, it would only prove that your piety was not worth having. If you cannot stand a few jokes and jeers, you are not built together in that habitation of God which He has made fireproof.

Bear up, and in the end you will find that this hard lot of yours, this severe discipline, did you a great deal of good to make you a better man than you ever would have been if you had been pampered in the lap of piety and kept from the battle. In later years your high and eminent post of usefulness may be, perhaps, owing to the severe and harsh discipline to which you were put in your younger days. *It is good for a man to bear the yoke in his youth* (Lamentations 3:27).

Or, perhaps, I am speaking to some one who has met with opposition from his own ungodly relatives. Remember how Jesus said, *"I came to send fire on the earth, and how I wish it were already kindled?...From now on five in one house will be divided: three against two and two against three"* (Luke 12:49, 52). Perhaps your father has threatened you, or better still, your husband has threatened to discard you. Now indeed you are walking through the fires. He rails at your godliness, makes mockery of everything you love, and does his best by cruelty to break your heart. My dear sister in Christ, you shall not be burned by the fire. If grace be in your heart, the devil can't drive it out, much less your husband.

If the Lord has called you by His grace, all the men on earth and all the fiends in hell can't reverse the calling. You shall find in the end you have not suffered any loss. The flame has not kindled upon you. You shall go through the fire and bless God for it. From a dying bed, or through the gates of paradise, you shall look back upon that dark pathway and say it was well for me that I had to carry that cross, so that now I am permitted to wear this crown.

9

The Evils of Sloth

A man cannot be idle and yet have Christ's sweet company. Christ is a quick walker. When His people want to talk with Him, they must also travel quickly, or else they will soon lose His company. Christ, my Master, goes about doing good, and if you would walk with Him you must go about upon the same mission. The Almighty Lover of the souls of men does not want to keep company with idle persons.

I find in Scripture that most of the great appearances that were made to eminent saints were made when they were busy. Moses was tending his father's flock when he saw the burning bush. Joshua was going around about the city of Jericho when he met the angel of the Lord. Jacob was in prayer and the angel of God appeared to him. Gideon was threshing, and Elisha was plowing, when the Lord called them. Matthew was collecting customs when he was bidden to follow Jesus, and James and John were fishing. The manna which the children of Israel kept unil morning bred worms and stank. Idle grace would soon become active corruption.

Moreover, sloth hardens the conscience. Laziness is one of the irons with which the heart is seared. Abimelech hired vain, light persons to serve his turn, and the prince of darkness does the same. Friends, it is a sad thing to rust the edge off from one's mind and to lose keenness of moral perception, but sloth will surely do this for us.

David felt the emasculating power of sloth. He was losing the force of his conscience and was ready for anything. The worst is near at hand. He walks upon the housetop and sees the object which excites his lust. He sends for the woman. The deed is done. It leads to another crime. He tempts Uriah. It leads to murder. Uriah is put to death so he can take Uriah's wife. Ah, David! How the mighty are fallen! How is the prince of Israel fallen and become like the lewd fellows who riot in the evening! From this day forth his sunshine turned to cloud, his peace gave place to suffering, and he went to his grave an afflicted and troubled man, who, though he could say, *"He has made with me an everlasting covenant,"* yet he had to precede it with that very significant clause, *"Although my house is not so with God"* (2 Samuel 23:5).

Is there anyone among the Lord's people who would crucify the Lord afresh and put Him to an open shame? Is there anyone that would wish to sell his Master with Judas, or turn aside from Christ with Demas? It is an easy accomplishment. You say you could not do it. Now, perhaps, you could not, but get slothful. Just do not fight the Lord's battles, and it will become not only easy for you to sin, but you will surely become its victim.

Oh, how Satan delights to make God's people fall into sin! Then, as it were, he thrusts another nail into the bloody hand of Christ. Then he stains the fair white linen of Christ's own garment. Then he vaunts himself that he has gotten a victory over the Lord Jesus and has led one of the Master's favorites captive at his will! If we would not thus make hell ring with satanic laughter and make the men of God weep because the cedars of Lebanon are cut down, let us watch unto prayer and be diligent in our Master's business, *"fervent in spirit, serving the Lord"* (Romans 12:11).

David was saved. I only speak to you who are saved, and I beg and beseech of you to take notice of David's fall and of the sloth that was at the beginning of it as a warning to yourselves. Some temptations come to the industrious, but all temptations attack the idle. Notice the invention used by country people to catch wasps. They will put a little sweet liquor into a long, narrow-necked vial. The do-nothing wasp comes by, smells the sweet liquor, plunges in, and is drowned. But the bee comes by, and, if she does stop for a moment to smell, yet she does not enter because she has honey of her own to make. She is too busy in the work of the commonwealth to indulge herself with the tempting sweets.

Master Greenham, a Puritan clergyman, was once counseling a woman who was greatly tempted. Upon making inquiries into her way of life, he found she had little to do. Greenham said, "That is the secret of your being so much tempted. Sister, if you are very busy, Satan may tempt you, but he will not easily prevail, and he will soon give up the attempt." Idle

Christians are not tempted by the devil so much as they do tempt the devil to tempt them. Idleness sets the door of the heart ajar and asks Satan to come in. But if we are occupied from morning until night, if Satan would get in, he must break through the door. Under sovereign grace and next to faith, there is no better shield against temptation than being *"not lagging in diligence, fervent in spirit, serving the Lord"* (Romans 12:11).

Let me remind those who are doing little for Christ, that once you were not so cold as this. There was a time with David when the sound of the clarion of war would have stirred his blood, and he would have been eager for the fray. There was a day when the very sight of Israel marshaled in regimental formation would have made David bold as a lion. Oh, it is an ill thing to see the lion changed like this! God's hero stays at home with the women!

There was a time when you would have gone over hedge and ditch to hear a sermon and never minded standing in the aisles, but now the sermons are tedious to some of you, although you have soft cushions to sit upon. Then if there was a house meeting or street witnessing, you were there. You say that was wildfire. Blessed wildfire! The Lord give you the wildfire back again. Even if it is wildfire, it is better to have wildfire than no fire at all. It is better to be called a fanatic than deserve to be called a drone in Christ's hive.

10

At the Siege of Copenhagen

A naval officer tells the following singular story concerning the siege of Copenhagen under Lord Nelson. An officer in the fleet said, "I was particularly impressed with an object which I saw three or four days after the terrific bombardment of that place. For several nights before the surrender, the darkness was ushered in with a tremendous roar of guns and mortars, accompanied by the whizzing of those destructive and burning engines of warfare, Congreve's rockets. The dreadful effects were soon visible in the brilliant lights through the city. The blazing houses of the rich and the burning cottages of the poor illuminated the heavens. And the wide-spreading flames, reflecting on the water, showed a forest of ships assembled around the city for its destruction. This work of conflagration went on for several nights, but the Danes at length surrendered.

"Some days after, on walking among the ruins, consisting of the cottages of the poor, houses of the rich, factories, lofty steeples, and humble meeting houses, I spotted a solitary unharmed house amid this barren field of desolation. All around it a burnt mass, this alone stood untouched by the fire, a monument of mercy. 'Whose house is that?' I asked.

"'That,' said the interpreter, 'belongs to a Quaker. He would neither fight nor leave his house, but remained in prayer with his family during the whole bombardment.'

"'Surely,' I mused, 'it is well with the righteous. God has been a shield to you in battle, a wall of fire round about you, a very present help in time of need. It might seem to be an invention of mine, only that it happens to be as authentic a piece of history as any that can be found.'"

There is another similar story told about that Danish war. Soon after the surrender of Copenhagen to the English, in the year 1807, detachments of soldiers were stationed in the surrounding villages for a time. It happened one day that three soldiers, belonging to a Highland regiment, were set to forage among the neighboring farmhouses. They went to several, but found them stripped and deserted. At length they came to a large garden, or orchard, full of apple trees, bending under the weight of fruit. They entered by a gate and followed a path which brought them to a neat farmhouse. Everything without spoke quietness and security. But, as they entered by the front door, the mistress of the house and her children ran screaming out by the back. The interior of the house presented an appearance of order and comfort superior to what might be expected from people in that station and from the habits of the country folk. A watch hung by the side of the fireplace, and a neat, well-filled bookcase attracted the attention of the elder soldier. He took down a book. It was written in a language unknown to him, but the name of Jesus Christ was legible on every page.

At this moment the master of the house entered by the door through which his wife and children had just fled. One of the soldiers, by threatening signs, demanded provisions. The man stood firm and undaunted, but shook his head. The soldier who held the book approached him, and pointing to the name of Jesus Christ, laid his hand upon his heart and looked up to heaven. Instantly the farmer grasped his hand, shook it vehemently, and then ran out of the room. Accompanied by his wife and children, he soon returned, laden with milk, eggs, and bacon which were freely tendered. When money was offered in return, it was at first refused. But as two of the soldiers were pious men, they, much to the chagrin of their companion, insisted upon paying for all they received.

When taking leave, the pious soldiers intimated to the farmer that it would be well for him to secrete his watch. By the most significant signs, he made them understand that he feared no evil, for his trust was in God. Though his neighbors on the right hand and on the left had fled from their habitations, and by foraging parties had lost what they could not remove, not a hair of his head had been injured, nor had he even lost an apple from his trees. The man knew that *"all who take the sword will perish by the sword"* (Matthew 26:52), so he just tried the non-resistant principle. God, in whom he put implicit confidence, would not let him be injured.

Remarkably, in the massacre of the Protestants in Ireland a long time ago, thousands of Quakers were in the country, but only two of them were killed. Those two had no faith in their own principles: one of them ran away and hid himself in the country, and the other kept arms in his house. But the others, unarmed, walked amid infuriated soldiers, both Roman Catholics and Protestants, and were never touched because they were strong in the strength of Israel's God. They put their swords into their scabbards, knowing that to war against another cannot be right.

Christ has said, *"Resist not an evil person. But whoever slaps you on your right cheek, turn the other to him also"* (Matthew 5:39). *"Love your enemies ...[be] kind to the unthankful and to the evil"* (Luke 6:35). *"Bless those that curse you, do good to those that hate you, and pray for those that spitefully use you and persecute you"* (Matthew 5:44). But we are ashamed to do that. We do not like it. We are afraid to trust God. Until we do it, we shall not know the majesty of faith, nor prove the power of God for our protection. *"My soul, wait silently for God alone, for my expectation is from Him"* (Psalm 62:5).

82

11

Sleep, a Gift of God

The sleep of the body is the gift of God. So said Homer of old when he described it as descending from the clouds and resting on the tents of the warriors around old Troy. So sang Virgil when he spoke of Palinurus falling asleep upon the prow of the ship. Sleep is the gift of God. We think that we lay our heads upon our pillows and compose our bodies in a peaceful posture, and, therefore, we naturally and necessarily sleep. But it is not so. Sleep is the gift of God. Not a man would close his eyes in slumber if God did not put His fingers on his eyelids. Did not the Almighty send a soft and balmy influence over his frame which lulled his thoughts into quiescence, making him enter into that blissful state of rest which we call sleep?

True, there are some drugs and narcotics by which men can poison themselves into near-death states and then call it sleep. However, the sleep of the healthy body is the gift of God. The Lord of love bestows it. His tenderness rocks the cradle for us every night. His kindness draws the curtain of darkness about us and bids the sun cover His blazing lamp. Love comes and says, "Sleep sweetly, my child. I give you sleep."

Have you not known what it is at times to lie upon your bed and strive in vain to slumber? As it is said of Darius, so might it be said of you: *"The king went to his palace and spent the night fasting... Also his sleep went from him"* (Daniel 6:18). You have attempted to seize sleep, but it escaped you. The more you tried to sleep the more surely were you awake. It is beyond our power to procure a healthy repose. You imagine if you fix your mind upon a certain subject until it engrosses your attention, you will then sleep, but you find yourself unable to do so. Ten thousand things drive through your brain as if the whole earth were whirling before you. You see all the things you have ever beheld dancing in wild confusion before your eyes. You close your eyes, but still you see. There are things in your ears and mind which will not let you be quiet. Sleep has forsaken the bed on which you court its power.

It is God alone who seals up the sea-boy's eyes upon the giddy mast and also gives the monarch rest. For with all aids and means to boot, the king could not sleep without the help of God, but would toss about, envying his slave to whom sheer weariness has become the friendly adminis-trator of slumber. It is God who steeps the mind in Lethe and bids us sleep so that our bodies may be refreshed, and so that for tomorrow's toil we may rise recruited and strengthened.

How thankful should we be for sleep! Sleep is the best physician that I know of. Sleep has healed more pains of wearied heads, hearts, and bones than the most eminent physicians upon earth. It is the best medicine, the choicest thing of all the names which are written in all the lists of pharmacy. No magic draught of the physi-cian can match with sleep. What a mercy it is that it belongs alike to all! God does not make sleep the boon of the rich man. He does not give it merely to the noble or the rich, so that they can monopolize it as a peculiar luxury for themselves. But He bestows it upon the poorest and most obscure, too.

Yet, if there be a difference, the sleep of the laboring man is sweet, whether he eats little or much. He who toils hardest sleeps all the more soundly for his work. While luxurious effeminacy cannot rest, tossing itself from side to side upon a bed of eiderdown, the hard-working laborer, with his strong and powerful limbs worn out and tired, throws himself upon his hard couch and sleeps. Upon waking, he thanks God that he has been refreshed.

You know not how much you owe to God, that He gives you rest at night. If you had sleepless nights, you would then value the blessing. If for weeks you lay tossing on your weary bed, you then would thank God for this favor. As sleep is the merciful appointment of God, it is a gift most precious, one that cannot be valued until it is taken away. Even then we cannot appreciate it as we ought.

The psalmist says there are some men who are so foolish as to deny themselves sleep. For purposes of gain or ambition, they rise up early and sit up late. We may have been guilty of the same thing. We have risen early in the morning that we might turn over the ponderous volume, in order to acquire knowledge. We have sat at night until our burned-out lamp has chided us and told us that the sun was rising. Our eyes have ached, our brain has throbbed, our heart has palpitated. We have been weary and worn out. We have risen early and sat up late, and have in that way come to eat the bread of sorrow by failing health and depressed spirits. Many of you business men are toiling in that fashion. We do not condemn you for it. We do not forbid rising early and sitting up late, but we remind you of this text: *"It is vain for you to rise up early, to sit up late, to eat the bread of sorrows: for so He gives His beloved sleep."* (Psalm 127:2).

Sleep is frequently used in a bad sense in the Word of God, to express the condition of carnal and worldly men. Some men have the sleep of carnal ease and sloth. Solomon tells us that they are unwise sons who slumber in the harvest, causing shame. When the harvest is spent and the summer is ended, they are not saved. (See Proverbs 10:5.)

Sleep often expresses a state of sloth, of deadness, of indifference, in which all ungodly men are found, according to the words, *"Let us not sleep as others do...but let us who are of the day be sober"* (1 Thessalonians 5:6, 8). *"It is high time for us to awake out of sleep"* (Romans 13:11). There are many who are sleeping the sluggard's sleep, who are tossing upon the bed of indolent ease. An awful awakening awaits them when they shall find that the time of their probation has been wasted, that the golden sands of their life have dropped unheeded from the hourglass, and that they have come into that world where there are no acts of pardon passed, no hope, no refuge, no salvation.

In other places you find sleep used as the figure of carnal security, in which so many are found. Look at Saul, lying asleep in fleshly surety. He is not like David, who said, *"I will both lie down in peace and sleep, for You alone, O Lord, make me dwell in safety"* (Psalm 4:8). Abner, the captain of Saul's host, was there, and all the troops lay around him. Sleep on, Saul! Abishai is standing at your pillow with a spear in his hand as he says, *"Let me strike him at once with the spear, right to the earth"* (1 Samuel 26:8). Still Saul sleeps. He knows not that he is on the brink of the eternal sleep!

Such are many of you, sleeping in jeopardy of your souls. Satan is standing over you, the law is ready to strike, vengeance is prepared. Even providence seems to say, "Shall I strike him? I will strike him but this once, and he shall never wake again." Jesus, the interposer, cries, "Stay, vengeance, stay." The spear is even now quivering. "Stay! Spare the sleeper yet another year, in the hope that he may yet awake from this long sleep of sin."

Like Sisera, I tell you, sinner, you are sleeping in the tent of the destroyer. You may have eaten butter out of a lordly dish, but you are sleeping on the doorstep of hell. Even now the enemy is lifting up the hammer and nail to strike you through your temples and pin you to the earth, that there you may lie forever in the death of everlasting torment which is so much worse than common death.

Also mentioned in Scripture is a sleep of lust, like that which Samson had when he lost his locks. Such is the sleep many have when they indulge in sin and wake to find themselves stripped, lost, and ruined. There is also the sleep of negligence such as the virgins had, about which it is said, *they all slumbered and slept*" (Matthew

25:5). Scripture refers to the sleep of sorrow which overcame Peter, James, and John in the garden of Gethsemane. But none of these are the gifts of God. They are incident to the frailty of our nature. They come upon us because we are fallen men. They creep over us because we are the sons of a lost and ruined parent. These sleeps are not the blessings of God, nor does He bestow them on His beloved.

12

An Innkeeper's Prayer

I t is said that Rowland Hill once had to put up in a village where there was no other house to stay at but a tavern. Having a pair of horses to care for and going into the best room of the inn, he was considered to be a valuable guest for the night. So the host came in and said, "Glad to see you, Mr. Hill." "I am going," was the reply, "to stay with you tonight. Will you let me have family prayer tonight in this house?" "I never had such a thing as family prayer here," said the landlord, "and I don't want to have it now." "Very well, just fetch my horses. I can't stop in a house where they won't pray to God. Bring the horses out."

Now, since Hill was too good a guest to lose, the man thought better of it and promised to have family prayer. "Ah, but," said Hill, "I'm not in the habit of conduct-ing prayer in other people's houses. You must conduct it yourself." The man said he could not pray. "But you must," replied Rowland Hill. "Oh, but I never did pray." "Then, my dear man, you will begin to-night," was the answer.

So when the time came and the family were on their knees, "Now," said Rowland Hill, "every man prays in his own house. You must offer prayer tonight." "I can't pray, I can't," said the landlord. "What, man, you have had all these mercies today, and are you so ungrateful that you cannot thank God for them? Besides, what a wicked sinner you have been! Can't you tell God what a sinner you've been and ask Him for pardon?" The man began to cry, "I can't pray, Mr. Hill, I can't, indeed I can't." "Then tell the Lord you can't. Tell Him you can't pray," said Mr. Hill, "and ask Him to help you."

Down went the poor landlord on his knees. "O Lord, I can't pray. I wish I could." "Ah! You have begun to pray," said Rowland Hill, "You have begun to pray, and you will never stop. As soon as God has set you to pray, faint though it be, you will never leave off. Now I'll pray for you." And so he did. It was not long before the Lord was pleased, through that strange instrumentality, to break the landlord's hard heart and to bring him to Christ.

Now, I say if any of you can't pray, tell the Lord you can't. Ask Him to help you to pray. Ask Him to show you your need to be saved. If you can't pray, ask Him to give you everything that you need. Christ will make as well as take the message. He will put His own blood upon your prayer, and the Father will send down the Holy Ghost to you to give you more faith and more trust in Christ.

13

Capital Punishment

Some time ago an excellent lady sought an interview with me, with the object, as she said, of enlisting my sympathy upon the question of "anti-capital punishment." I heard the excellent reasons she urged against hanging men who had committed murder. Though they did not convince me, I did not seek to answer them. She proposed that when a man committed murder, he should be confined for life. My remark was that a great many men who had been confined half their lives were not a bit the better for it. As for her belief that they would necessarily be brought to repentance, I was afraid it was but a dream.

"Ah!" she said, good soul as she was, "that is because we have been all wrong about punishments. We punish people because we think they deserve to be punished. Now, we ought to show them that we love them, that we only punish to make them better."

"Indeed, madam," I said, "I have heard that theory a great many times, and I have seen much fine writing upon the matter, but I am no believer in it. The design of punishment should be amendment, but the ground of punishment lies in the positive guilt of the offender. I believe that when a man does wrong, he ought to be punished for it, and that there is a guilt in sin which justly merits punishment."

No, she could not see that. Sin was a very wrong thing, but punishment was not a proper idea. She thought that people were treated too cruelly in prison, and that they ought to be taught that we love them. If they were treated kindly in prison and tenderly dealt with, they would grow so much better, she was sure.

With a view of interpreting her own theory, I said, "I suppose, then, you would give criminals all sorts of indulgences in prison. Some great vagabond who has committed burglary dozens of times—I suppose you would let him sit in an easy chair in the evening before a nice fire, mix him a glass of spirits and water, give him his pipe, and make him happy to show him how much we love him."

"Well, no, I would not give him the spirits, but still, all the rest would do him good." I thought that was a delightful picture certainly. It seemed to me to be the most prolific method of cultivating rogues which ingenuity could invent. I imagine that you could grow any number of thieves in that way, for it would be a special means of propagating all manner of roguery and wickedness. These very delightful theories, to such a simple mind as mine, were the source of much amusement. The idea of fondling villains and treating their crimes as if they were the tumbles and falls of children made me laugh heartily. I fancied I saw the government resigning its functions to these excellent persons and the grand results of their marvelously kind experiments. The sword of the magistrate would be transformed into a soup spoon, and the jail would become a sweet retreat for injured reputations.

Little, however, did I think I would live to see this kind of nonsense taught in pulpits. I had no idea that there would come out a theology which would bring down God's moral government from the solemn aspect in which Scripture reveals it to a namby-pamby sentimentalism, which adores a Deity destitute of every masculine virtue. But we never know today what may occur tomorrow. We have lived to see a certain sort of men—thank God they are not Baptists, though I am sorry to say there are a great many Baptists who are beginning to follow in their trail—who seek to teach nowadays that God is a universal Father, and that our ideas of His dealing with the impenitent as a Judge, and not as a Father, are remnants of antiquated error.

Sin, according to these men, is a disorder rather than an offense, an error rather than a crime. Love is the only attribute they can discern, and the full-orbed Deity they have not known. Some of these men push their way very far into the bogs and mire of falsehood until they inform us that eternal punishment is ridiculed as a dream. In fact, books now appear which teach us that there is no such thing as the vicarious sacrifice of our Lord Jesus Christ. They use the word atonement, it is true, but in regard to its meaning they have removed the ancient landmark. They acknowledge that the Father has shown His great love to poor sinful man by sending

His Son. But they fail to admit that God was inflexibly just in the exhibition of His mercy, that He punished Christ on the behalf of His people, that God ever will punish anybody in His wrath, or that there is such a thing as justice apart from discipline. Even sin and hell are but old words employed henceforth in a new and altered sense. Those are old-fashioned notions, and we poor souls who go on talking about election and imputed righteousness are behind the times.

I have often thought the best answer for all these new ideas is that the true gospel was always preached to the poor. *"The poor have the gospel preached to them"* (Luke 7:22). I am sure that the poor will never learn the gospel of these new clerics for they cannot make head or tail of it, nor can the rich either. After you have read through one of their volumes, you do not have the least idea of what the book is about until you have read it through eight or nine times. Then you begin to think you are a very stupid being for ever having read such inflated heresy, for it sours your temper and makes you feel angry to see the precious truths of God trodden under foot. Some of us must stand against these attacks on truth, although we do not love controversy. We rejoice in the liberty of our fellow men and would have them proclaim their convictions. However, if they touch these precious things, they touch the apple of our eye. We can allow a thousand opinions in the world. But anything that infringes upon the precious doctrine of a covenant salvation through the imputed righteousness of our Lord Jesus Christ, against that we must enter our hearty and solemn protest, as long as God spares us. Take away once from us those glorious doctrines, and where are we, brethren?

We may lay down and die, for nothing remains that is worth living for. We have come to the valley of the shadow of death, when we find these doctrines to be untrue. If these things are not the verities of Christ, there is no comfort left for any poor man under God's sky, and it were better for us never to have been born. I may say what Jonathan Edwards says at the end of his book, "If any man could disprove the doctrines of the gospel, he should then sit down and weep to think they were not true, for it would be the most dreadful calamity that could happen to the world, to have a glimpse of such truths, and then for them to melt away in the thin air of fiction, as having no substantiality in them."

Stand up for the truth of Christ. I would not have you be bigoted, but I would have you be decided. Do not give countenance to any of this trash and error which is going abroad, but stand firm. Be not turned away from your steadfastness by any pretense of intellectuality and high philosophy, but earnestly contend for the faith once delivered to the saints. Hold fast to the sound words which you have heard from us and have been taught, even as you have read in the Book which is the way of everlasting life.

14

Rowland Hill and Lady Erskine

Once when Rowland Hill was preaching, Lady Ann Erskine happened to be driving by. She was in the outer ring of the circle, and she asked the coachman what all the people were there for. He replied, "They are going to hear Rowland Hill."

Well, she had heard a great deal about this strange man, accounted to be the very wildest of preachers, and so she drew near.

No sooner did Rowland Hill see her, than he said, "Come, I am going to have an auction. I am going to sell Lady Ann Erskine." Of course, she stopped to find out how she was going to be disposed of.

"Who will buy her?" Up came the world. "What will you give for her?" The world offered, "I will give her all the pomp and vanities of this present life. She shall be a happy woman here, she shall be very

101

rich, she shall have many admirers, and she shall go through this world with many joys." "You shall not have her. Her soul is an everlasting thing. It is a poor price you are offering. You are only giving a little, and what shall it profit her if she gain the whole world and lose her own soul?"

Here came another purchaser—here was the devil. "What will you give for her?" "Well," said he, "I will let her enjoy the pleasures of sin for a season. She shall indulge in everything her heart shall set itself unto. She shall have everything to delight the eye and the ear. She shall indulge in every sin and vice that can possibly give a transient pleasure." "Ah, Satan! What will you do for her forever? You shall not have her, for I know what you are. You would give a paltry price for her, and then destroy her soul for all eternity."

But then came another bidder. "I know Him," Hill said, "It is the Lord Jesus. What will You give for her?" Says he, "It is not what I will give. It is what I have given. I have given My life, My blood for her. I have bought her with a price, and I will give her heaven forever and ever. I will give her grace in her heart now and glory through out eternity."

"O Lord Jesus Christ," said Rowland Hill, "You shall have her. Lady Erskine, do you object to the bargain?" She was fairly caught. There was no answer that could be given. "It is done," he said, "It is done. You are the Savior's. I have betrothed you unto Him. Never break that contract." And she never did. From that time forth, from being a gay and volatile woman, she became one of the most serious persons, one of the greatest supporters of the truth of the gospel in those times and died in a glorious and certain hope of entering the kingdom of heaven.

Whosoever is willing to have Christ, Christ is willing to have him.

15

God Speaking to All

Every man in his calling has a sermon preached to him. The farmer has a thousand sermons. He need not go an inch without hearing the songs of angels and the voice of spirits wooing him to righteousness, for all nature around about him has a tongue given to it, whenever man has an ear to hear.

There are others, however, engaged in a business which allows them to see but very little of nature, and yet even there God has provided them with a lesson. The baker provides us with our bread. He thrusts his fuel into the oven, causing it to glow with heat, and puts bread in. Well may he, if he is an ungodly man, tremble as he stands at the oven's mouth, for there is a text which he may well comprehend as he stands there: *"For, behold, the day is coming, burning like an oven, and all the proud, yes, all who do wickedly will be stubble. And the day that is coming will burn them up...They gather them and throw them into the fire, and they are burned"* (Malachi 4:1; John 15:6). Out of the oven's mouth comes a hot and burning warning. The man's heart might melt like wax within him if he would but regard it.

Then see the butcher. How does the beast speak to him? He sees the lamb almost lick his knife, and the bullock goes unconsciously to the slaughter. How might he think every time that he strikes the unconscious animal who knows nothing of death or his own doom! Are we not, all of us who are without Christ, fattening for the slaughter? Are we not more foolish than the bullock, for does not the wicked man follow his executioner and walk after his own destroyer into the very chambers of hell? When we see a drunkard pursuing his drunkenness, or an unchaste man running in the way of licentiousness, is he not as an ox going to the slaughter, until a dart pierces him through the liver? Has not God sharpened his knife and made ready his axe, that the fatlings of this earth may be killed? Then He shall say to the fowls of the air and the beasts of the field, "Behold,

I have made a feast of vengeance for you, and you shall feast upon the blood of the slain and make yourselves drunken with the streams." (See Ezekiel 39:17-19.) Aye, butcher, there is a lecture for you in your trade, and your business may reproach you.

Shoemaker, you whose craft is to sit still all day fashioning shoes for our feet! The stone in your lap may reproach you, for your heart is perhaps as hard as that. Have you not been convicted often at your lapstone, and yet your heart has never been broken or melted? What shall the Lord say to you at last, when, your stony heart being still within you, He shall condemn you and cast you away because you would have none of His rebukes and would not turn at the voice of His exhortation?

Let the brewer remember that as he brews, he must drink. Let the potter tremble that he is like a vessel marred upon the wheel. Let the printer take heed that his life is set in heavenly type and not in the black letter of sin. Painter, beware! Paint will not suffice. We must have unvarnished realities.

Or you engaged in business, where you are continually using scales and measures, might you not often put yourselves into those scales? Might you not fancy you saw the great Judge standing by with His gospel in one scale and you in the other, as He solemnly looks down upon you and says, *"MENE, MENE, TEKEL...You have been weighed in the balances, and found wanting"* (Daniel 5:25, 27). Some of you use the measure, and when you have measured out, you cut off the portion that your customer requires. Think of your life, too. It is to be of a certain length. Every year brings the measure a little farther, until at last there come the scissors that shall clip off your life, and it will be done. How do you know when you have come to the last inch? What is that disease you have but the first snip of the scissors? What is that trembling in your bones, that failing in your eyesight, that fleeing of your memory, that departure of your youthful vigor, but the first tear? How soon will you be torn in two, the remnant of your days past away, and your years all numbered and gone, misspent and wasted forever?

But you say you are engaged as a servant and your occupations are diverse. Then diverse are the lectures God preaches to you. *"Like a servant who earnestly desires the shade, and like a hired man who eagerly looks for his wages"* (Job 7:2). There is a similarity for you, when you have fulfilled your day on earth and shall take your wages at last. Who then is your master? Are you serving Satan and the lusts of the flesh, and will you take out your wages at last in the hot metal of destruction? Or are you serving the fair Prince Emmanuel, and shall your wages be the golden crowns of heaven? Oh, happy are you if you serve a good Master! For according to your master shall be your reward. As is your labor, such shall the end be.

Are you one that guides the pen, and from hour to hour wearily you write? Ah, man! Know that your life is a writing. When your hand is not on the pen, you are a writer still. You are always writing upon the pages of eternity. Either you are writing your sins, or else your holy confidence in Him that loved you. Happy shall it be for you, writer, if your name is written in the Lamb's book of life, and if that black writing of yours during your pilgrimage below shall have been blotted out with the red blood of Christ, and you shall have written upon you the fair name of Jehovah to stand legible forever.

Or perhaps you are a physician or a chemist. You prescribe or prepare medicines for man's body. God stands there by the side of your pestle and your mortar, and by the table where you write your prescriptions, and says to you, "Man, you are sick. I can prescribe for you. The blood and righteousness of Christ, laid hold of by faith and applied by the Spirit, can cure your soul. I can compound a medicine for you that shall rid you of your ills and bring you to the place where the inhabitants shall no more say, 'I am sick.' Will you take My medicine, or will you reject it? Is it bitter to you, and do you turn away from it? Come, drink, My child, drink, for your life lies here. *How shall [you] escape if [you] neglect so great a salvation?*" (Hebrews 2:3).

Do you cast iron, melt lead, or fuse the hard metals of the mines? Then pray that the Lord may melt your heart and cast you in the mold of the gospel. Do you make garments for men? Oh, be careful that you find a garment for yourself forever. Are you busy in building all day long, laying one stone upon the other and the mortar in the crevice? Then remember you are building for eternity, too. Oh, that you may yourself be built upon a good foundation! Oh, that you may build on that solid rock, not wood or hay or stubble, but gold and silver and precious stones—things that will abide the fire! Take care, man, lest you should be God's scaffold, lest you should be used on earth to be a scaffolding for building His church, and when his church is built you should be cast down and burned up with fire unquenchable. Take heed that you are built upon a rock, and not upon the sand, and that the crimson cement of the Savior's precious blood unites you to the foundation of the building and to every stone thereof.

Are you a jeweller, and do you cut your gems and polish diamonds from day to day? Oh, that you would take warning from the contrast which you present to the stone on which you exercise your craft! You cut it, and it glitters the more you cut it. But though you have been cut and ground— though you have had cholera and fever and have been at death's door many a day—you are none the brighter, but rather the duller, Alas! You are no diamond. You are but a pebble of the brook. In that day when God makes up His jewels, He shall not enclose you in the casket of His treasures, for you are not one of the precious sons of Zion, comparable to fine gold.

Be your situation what it may, be your calling what it may, there is a continual sermon preached to your conscience. I hope that you would now from this time forth open both your eyes and ears, and see and hear the things that God would teach you.

16

The Suspected Inn

Poor Ananias was afraid to go to Saul. He thought it was very much like stepping into a lion's den. "If I go to his house," he reasoned, "the moment he sees me, he will take me to Jerusalem at once, for I am one of Christ's disciples. I dare not go." God says, "Behold, he prays." "Well," says Ananias, "that is enough for me. If he is a praying man, he will not hurt me. If he is a man of real devotion, I am safe."

Be sure, you may always trust a praying man. I do not know how it is, but even ungodly men pay a reverence to a sincere Christian. A master likes to have a praying servant after all. If he does not regard religion himself, he likes to have a pious servant, and will trust him rather than any other. True, there are some of your professedly praying people that have not a bit of prayer in them; but whenever you find a really praying man, you may trust him with untold gold. If he really prays, you need not be afraid of him. The person who communes with God in secret may be trusted in public. I always feel safe with a man who is a visitor to the mercy seat.

I have heard an anecdote of two gentlemen traveling together, somewhere in Switzerland. Presently they came into the midst of the forests. You know the gloomy tales the people are inclined to tell about the inns in the lone places—how dangerous it is to lodge in them. One of the travelers, an infidel, said to the other, who was a Christian, "I don't like stopping here at all. It is a very queer-looking house." "Well," said the other, "let us try." So they went into the house, but it looked so suspicious that neither of them were comfortable. No doubt they would have greatly preferred being at home in England.

Presently the landlord said, "Gentlemen, I always read and pray with my family before going to bed. Will you allow me to do so tonight?" "Yes," they said, "with the greatest pleasure." When they went upstairs, the infidel said, "I am not at all afraid now." "Why?" said the Christian. "Because our host has prayed." "Oh!" said the other, "then it seems, after all, you think something of religion. Because a man prays, you can go to sleep in his house without fear of being robbed or murdered." And it was marvelous how both of them did sleep. Sweet dreams they had, for they felt that where the house had been roofed by prayer and walled with devotion, none would do them harm. This, then, was the argument for Ananias, to convince him that he might go with safety to Saul's lodging.

Mrs. Berry used to say, "I would not be hired out of my prayer closet for a thousand worlds." Mr. Jay said, "If the twelve apostles were living near you, and you had access to them, they would prove a real injury to your souls if your relationship drew you from the closet." Prayer is the ship which brings home the richest freight from the celestial shores. Prayer is the soil which yields the most abundant harvest.

Brother, when you rise in the morning, your business is so pressing that, with a hurried word or two, out you go into the world. At night, jaded and tired, you give God the remnants of the day. The consequence is that you have no communion with Him.

The reason we do not have more true religion among us now is because we do not have more secret prayer. Sirs, I have no opinion of the churches of the present day that do not pray. Say to your minister, "Sir, we must have more prayer." Urge the people to more prayer. Have a prayer meeting, even if you have it all to yourself. If you are asked how many were present, you can say, "Four." "Four! How so?" "Why, there was myself, and God the Father, God the Son, and God the Holy Ghost. We have had a rich and real communion together."

We must have an outpouring of real devotion, or else what is to become of many of our churches? Oh, may God awaken us all and stir us up to pray, for when we pray, we shall be victorious! I should like to take you, as Samson did the foxes, tie the fire brands of prayer to you, and send you in among the shocks of corn, until you set the whole field ablaze. I should like to make a conflagration by my words and set all the churches on fire with zeal for God's glory.

17

Some Popular Errors

Many imagine that salvation cannot be accomplished except in some undefinable and mysterious way, and the minister and the priest are mixed up with it. Hear, then! If you had never seen a minister in your lives, if you had never heard the voice of the bishop or an elder of the church, yet if you did call on the name of the Lord, your salvation would be quite as sure without those as with one.

We are all clergy who love the Lord Jesus Christ, and you are as much fit to preach the gospel, if God has given you the ability and called you to the work by his Spirit, as any man alive. No priestly hand, no hand of presbytery, no ordination of men is necessary. We stand upon the rights of manhood to speak what we believe, and next to that we stand upon the call of God's Spirit in the heart bidding us to testify of

His truth. But neither Paul nor an angel from heaven, nor Apollos, nor Cephas, can help you in salvation. It is not of man, neither by men. And neither Pope, nor Archbishop, nor bishop, nor priest, nor minister, nor anyone has any grace to give to others. We must each of us go ourselves to the Fountainhead, pleading this promise, *"Whoever calls on the name of the LORD shall be saved"* (Romans 10:13). If I were shut up in the mines of Siberia, where I could never hear the gospel, I still could call upon the name of Christ and be saved. The road is just as straight without the minister as with him. The path to heaven is just as clear from the wilds of Africa and from the dens of the jailhouse or the dungeon, as it is from the sanctuary of God.

Nevertheless, for edification, all Christians love the ministry, though not for salvation. Though neither in priest nor preacher do they trust, yet the word of God is sweet to them. *"How beautiful upon the mountains are the feet of him who brings good news, who proclaims peace"* (Isaiah 52:7).

Another very common error is that a good dream is considered a most splendid thing in order to save people. Some of you do not know the extent to which this error prevails. I happen to know it. It is received among many persons that if you dream you see the Lord in the night, you will be saved. Also, if you can see Him on the cross, or if you think you see some angels, or if you dream that God says to you, "You are forgiven," all is well. However, if you do not have a very nice dream, you cannot be saved, or so some people think. Now, if this is correct, the sooner we all begin to eat opium the better because there is nothing that makes people dream so much as that. The best advice I could give would be: let every minister generously distribute opium, and then his people would all dream themselves into heaven.

Out with that rubbish! There is nothing in it. Dreams—the disordered fabrics of a wild imagination, often the totterings of the fair pillars of a grand conception—how can they be the means of salvation? You know Rowland Hill's good answer. I must quote it for lack of a better. When a woman pleaded that she was saved because she dreamed, he said, "Well, my good woman, it is very nice to have good dreams when you are asleep, but I want to see how you act when you are awake. If your conduct is not consistent in religion when you are awake, I will not give a snap of the finger for your dreams."

Ah! I do marvel that ever any person should go to such a depth of ignorance as to tell me the stories that I have heard myself about dreams. Poor dear creatures! When they were sound asleep, they saw the gates of heaven opened, a white angel came and washed their sins away, they saw that they were pardoned, and they have never had a doubt or a fear since then. It is time that you should begin to doubt, a very good time that you should; for if that is all the hope you have, it is a poor one. Remember, it is *"whoever **calls** upon the name of the LORD,"* not whoever dreams about Him.

Dreams may do some good. Sometimes people have been frightened out of their senses by them. They were better out of their senses than they were in, for they did more mischief when they were in their senses than they did when they were out. The dreams did good in that sense.

Some people, too, have been alarmed by dreams, but to trust in them is to trust in a shadow, to build your hopes on bubbles which scarcely need a puff of wind to burst them into nothingness. Oh, remember, you want no vision, no marvelous appearance! If you have had a vision or a dream, you need not despise it, for it may have benefitted you. However, do not trust to it. But if you have had none, remember a dream is not the calling upon God's name to which the promise is appended.

There are some people who think they must have some very wonderful kind of feelings or some most extraordinary thoughts such as they never had before, or else certainly they cannot be saved. A woman once applied to me for admission to church membership. I asked her whether she had ever had a change of heart. She said, "Oh yes, sir, such a change! You know, I felt it across the chest so singularly, sir. When I was praying one day, I did not know what was the matter with me, I felt so different. And when I went to the chapel, sir, one night, I came away and felt so different from what I felt before, so light." "Yes", I said, "light-headed, my dear soul, that is what you felt, but nothing more, I am afraid." The good woman was sincere enough. She thought it was all right with her because something had affected her lungs, or in some way stirred her physical frame.

"No," I hear you say, "people cannot be so stupid as this." I assure you that there are many that have no better hope of heaven than that, for I am dealing with a very popular objection just now. "I thought," said one, addressing me one day, "I thought when I was in the garden, surely Christ could take my sins away just as easily as He could move the clouds. Do you know, sir, in a moment or two the cloud was all gone, and the sun was shining. Thought I to myself, the Lord is blotting out my sin." Such a ridiculous thought as that, you say, cannot occur often. I tell you it does, very frequently indeed. People suppose that the most absurd nonsense in all the earth is a manifestation of divine grace in their hearts.

Now, the only feeling I ever want to have is just this: I want to feel that I am a sinner and that Christ is my Savior. You may keep your visions, ecstasies, raptures, and dancing to yourselves. The only feeling that I desire to have is deep repentance and humble faith. And if, poor sinner, you have got that, you are saved. Why, some people believe that before they can be saved there must be a kind of electric shock, some very wonderful thing that is to go all through them from head to foot. Now hear this, *"The word is near you, in your mouth and in your heart...If you confess with your mouth the Lord Jesus and believe in your heart that God has raised Him from the dead, you will be saved"* (Romans 10:8-9). What do you want with all this nonsense of dreams and supernatural thoughts? All that is necessary is that, as a guilty sinner, I should come and cast myself on Christ. That done, the soul is safe, and all the visions in the universe could not make it safer.

And now, I have one more error to try to rectify. Among very poor people—and I have visited some of them and know what I say to be true—among the very poor and uneducated, there is a very current idea that somehow or other salvation is connected with learning to read and write. You smile, perhaps, but I know it. Often has a poor woman said, "Sir, this is no good to poor, ignorant creatures like us. There is no hope for me, sir. I cannot read. Do you know, sir, I don't know a letter? I think if I could read a bit, I might be saved; but, ignorant as I am, I do not know how I can, for I have got no understanding, sir." I have found this in the country districts, too, among people who might learn to read if they liked. And there are none that cannot, unless they are lazy. Yet they sit down in cold indifference about salvation, under the notion that the parson could be saved because he reads a chapter so nicely, that the clerk could be saved for he said "Amen" so well, that the squire could be saved for he knew a great deal and had a vast many books in his library, but that they could not be saved for they did not know anything, and therefore it was impossible.

My poor friend, you do not want to know much to go to heaven. I would advise you to know as much as ever you can. Do not be backward in trying to learn. But in regards to going to heaven, the way is so plain, that *whoever walks the road, although a fool, shall not go astray*" (Isaiah 35:8).

18

Profit and Loss

It is astonishing for how little a man will sell his soul. I remember an anecdote that I believe is true—at least, I hope it is.

A minister, going across some fields, met a countryman and said to him, "Well, friend, it is a most delightful day."

The countryman agreed, "Yes, sir, it is."

Having spoken to him about the beauties of the scenery and so forth, the minister said, "How thankful we ought to be for our mercies! I hope you never come out without praying."

"Pray, sir?" the countryman responded, "Why, I never pray! I have got nothing to pray for."

"What a strange man!" said the minister, "Doesn't your wife pray?"

"If she likes."

"Don't your children pray?"

"If they like, they do."

"Well, you mean to say you do not pray," said the minister. (As I think, not very correctly, for no doubt he saw that the man was superstitious.) "Now, I will give you half-a-crown if you will promise me not to pray as long as you live."

"Very well," said the man, "I don't see what I have got to pray for." He took the half-crown. When he went home, the thought struck him, What have I done?

Something inside said to him, "Well, John, you will die soon, and you will want to pray then. You will have to stand before your Judge, and it will be a sad thing not to have prayed." Thoughts of this kind came over him, and he felt dreadfully miserable. The more he thought, the more miserable he felt. His wife asked him what was the matter. He could hardly tell her for some time. At last he confessed he had taken half-a-crown never to pray again, and that was preying on his mind.

The poor ignorant soul thought it was the evil one that had appeared to him. "Aye, John," his wife said, "sure enough, it was the devil, and you have sold your soul to him for that half-crown." The poor creature could not work for several days, and he became perfectly miserable from the conviction that he had sold himself to the evil one.

However, the minister knew what he was about. There was a barn close by, and he was going to preach there. He guessed the man would be there to ease his terror of mind. Sure enough, he was there one Sabbath evening. He heard the same man who gave him the half-crown take for his text these words: *"For what will it profit a man if he gains the whole world, and loses his own soul?"* (Mark 8:36). "Aye," said the minister, "what will it profit a man who sold his soul for half-a-crown?"

Up gets the man, crying out, "Sir, take it back! Take it back!"

"Why," said the minister, "You wanted the half-crown, and you said you did not need to pray."

"But, sir," he said, "I must pray. If I do not pray, I am lost." After some testing by parleying, the half-crown was returned, and the man was on his knees, praying to God. And it came to pass that this very circumstance was the means of saving his soul and making him a changed man.

19

The Avalanche and the Locusts

A present God! I cannot suggest a theme that may make you more full of courage in time a of danger and trouble. You will find it exceedingly helpful and consoling if you can discover God in your trifles. Our lives are made up of trifles. If we had a God only for the great things and not for the little things, we should be miserable indeed.

If we had a God of the temple, and not a God of the tents of Jacob, where would we be? But, blessed be our heavenly Father, He that wings an angel, guides a sparrow. He that rolls a world along, molds a tear and marks its orbit when it trickles from its source. There is a God in the motion of a grain of dust blown by the summer wind, as much as in the revolutions of the stupendous planet. There is a

God in the sparkling of a firefly as truly as in the flaming comet. Carry with you, I beseech you, through your day the thought that God is there at your table, in your bedroom, in your workroom, and at your counter. Recognize the doing and being of God in every little thing.

Think for a moment, and you will find that there are many promises of Scripture giving the sweetest consolation in trivial matters. *"He shall give His angels charge over you, to keep you in all your ways. In their hands they shall bear you up"* (Psalm 91:11-12). Why? Lest you fall from a precipice or hurl yourself from a pinnacle? No, *"Lest you dash your foot against a stone!"* A small danger, but a great providence to ward us from it.

What else does Scripture say? Does it say, "The very days of your life are numbered"? It does not say so, though that were true. Rather, *"the very hairs of your head are all numbered"* (Matthew 10:30). Yet again, what does the Scripture say? Does it say, "The Lord knows the eagles, and not an eagle falls to the ground apart from your Father's will"? No, but, *"Are not two sparrows sold for a copper coin? And not one of them falls to the ground apart from your Father's will"* (Matthew 10:29). He is a great God in little things.

I am sure it will spare you much vexation if you will just remember this, for this is where our anxiety develops. We often get into a bad temper about a trifle, when a great trial does not agitate us. We are angry because we have scalded ourselves with a little water or have lost a button from our clothes. Yet the greatest calamity can scarcely disturb us. You smile, because it is true. Job himself, who said, *"The LORD gave, and the LORD has taken away"* (Job 1:21), might have grown angry because of some rough edge in his potsherd. Take care that you see God in little things, that your mind may be always calm and composed, and that you are not foolish enough to allow a trifle to overcome a saint of God.

Our life is entirely dependent upon God. One sees strange sights in journeying, scenes which will never be erased from the memory. Some years ago, just under a tremendous rock, I saw a vast mass of broken stones and earth tossed about in wild confusion and raised in huge hillocks. My driver said to me, "That is the grave of a village."

Some years previous there lived upon that spot a joyful and happy people. They went forth to their daily work, they ate and drank as men do to this day. One day they saw a great crack in the mountain that hung overhead. They heard alarming noises, but they had heard such sounds before. The old men said that there might be something coming, but they were not sure. Suddenly, however, without further notice, the whole side of the hill was in motion. Before the villagers could escape from their huts, the hamlet was buried beneath the fallen rocks. There it lies now. Neither bone of man nor piece of habitation has ever been discovered in the wreck. So thoroughly was everything crushed and buried that nothing, even by the most diligent search, could ever be discovered.

There are many villages standing in similar positions today. I passed another spot where there was a shelving mountain, with its layers slanting towards the valley. A town which had been built at the foot had been entirely covered and a lake filled up by one tremendous slide from the top of the hill. Yet, still there stand new houses, and men venture to live among the graves of their sires.

We are prone to say that these people ought to look up every morning and pray, "O Lord, spare this village!" Standing there, where they might be crushed in a moment, where the slightest motion of the earth within would bring down the hill upon them, they ought to lift up their hearts to the Preserving Ones and say, "Oh, You keeper of Israel, keep us both day and night."

Ah! You and I are in the same position. Though no jutting crags overhang our homesteads, though no mountain threatens to leap upon our city, yet are there a thousand gates to death. Other agencies besides these can hurry mortals to their tombs. You are sitting today as near to the jaws of death as those villagers who are dwelling there. Oh, if only you felt it! One breath choked up, and you are dead. Perhaps your life is a thousand times in danger every moment. As many times as there are ebbing and flowing of the blood, as many times as there is breathing from the lungs, so many times does your life hang in such jeopardy that it only needs your God to will it, and you fall dead in your seat and are carried out a pale, lifeless corpse.

There are parts of the mountain passes of the Alps of such danger to the traveler that when you traverse them in winter, the mule drivers muffle the bells of their beasts, lest the faintest sound should bring down an avalanche of snow and sweep you into the bottomless precipice beneath. One would think that there the traveler must feel that he is in God's hand.

You are in the same position now, though you do not see it. Just open the eyes of your spirit, and you may see the avalanche overhanging you today with the rock trembling to its fall at this very moment. Let your soul behold the latent lightnings that God conceals within His hand. You may soon see that to crush a gnat with your finger is not as easy for you to do as for God to take away your life now or whenever He pleases.

As it is with our lives, so is it with the comforts of life. What would life be without its comforts? Even more, what would it be without its necessaries? How absolutely dependent are we upon God for the bread which is the staff of life!

I never felt more truly the dependence of man upon his God than I did at the foot of the Alpine pass of the Splugen. I saw in the distance the whole road looked black, as if it had been spread over with heaps of black earth. As we neared it, we discovered it was a mass of locusts in full march—tens of thousands of myriads of them. As we drew nearer, they divided as regularly as if they had been an army and made room for the carriage. No sooner was it passed, than the ranks were filled up again, and they went on in their devouring march. On we went for several miles, and there was nothing to be seen except these creatures, literally covering the ground here and there in thick layers, like a shower of black snow.

Then I realized the meaning of the language of the prophet: *"The land is like the Garden of Eden before them, and behind them a desolate wilderness"* (Joel 2:3). They had eaten up every green blade. There stood the Indian corn with just the dry stems, but every green particle was gone. In the front of their march, you saw the vines beginning to ripen and the fields of grain hastening to perfection. There stood the poor cottager at his door. The wheat that he had planted and the vines that he had tended must all be eaten and devoured before his own eyes. The pastures were literally alive with these fiery creatures. When they first entered the field, there was green pasture for the cows of the poor cottagers. Let them stop there an hour, and you might take up the dust by handfuls and nothing left besides.

"Ah!" said my guide, "It is a sad thing for these poor people. In a month's time those creatures will be as big and as long as my finger, and then they will eat up the trees—the mulberry trees with which the poor men feed their silkworms and which furnish then with a little wealth. They will devour every green thing until there is nothing left but the bare, dry stems." In armies as countless as the sands of the sea and as fierce to look upon, they are well-described by the prophet Joel in his terrible picture of them, as *"His army, His camp is very great"* (Joel 2:11). I thought within myself, if God can thus sweep this valley and make a waste of it with these little creatures, what a mercy it is that He is a kind and gracious God, or else He might let loose the like on all the people of the earth, and then nothing would stare us in the face but famine, despair, and death!

We are not simply dependent upon God for the comforts, but for the power to enjoy the comforts. It is an evil which we have seen under the sun—men who had wealth, riches, and plenty, but who did not have the power to partake thereof. I have seen a man hungry and full of appetite, but no bread to eat. But I have seen a sight perhaps more sad: a man with food of the most luxurious kind to whom taste seemed denied, to whom every mouthful was a thing to be detested.

The Lord has but in His judgment to strike any of us with nervousness—that nervousness at which the strong may laugh, but which makes the weak tremble—and everything will become dark before us. He has but to affect some portion of your body, and you shall see no brightness in the sun. The very fields will lose their green intensity before you. The most happy event will only be a source of deeper gloom. You will look on everything through a dark glass, and see nothing but darkness and despair. He has but to touch you with sickness, and motion may be misery. Even to lie upon a bed may be a repetition of tortures as you toss from side to side. Worse still, the Lord has but to put His finger on your brain, and you become a raving lunatic or, what may seem better but is more despicable, a drivelling idiot. Oh, how little then has He to do to overturn your all, to pull down that mighty castle of your joys, and darken the windows of your hope!

Again, for life, for necessities, for comforts, you are as absolutely in the hand of God as the clay is in the hand of the potter. Your rebellion is but the writhing of a worm. You may murmur, but your murmurs cannot affect Him. You may ask your comrades to join in league with you against the Almighty God, but His purpose will stand fast, and you must submit.

20

How the World Gives

In first place, the world gives scantily. Even the world's best friends have had cause to complain of its scurvy treatment. When reading the biographies of mighty men whom the world honors, you will be soon convinced that the world is a most ungrateful friend. If you should devote your whole life to serving the world and making it happy, think not the world would ever return you so much as a penny.

Robert Burns is an instance of the world's fine gratitude. He was the world's beloved poet. He sang about the roaring tankards' foaming. He sang about the loves of women and the joys of lust. The world admired him, but what did the world do for him? He dragged along his whole life in almost poverty.

When the time came for Robert Burns to be honored (which was all too late for a buried man), how did they honor him? He had poor relatives. Look to the subscription list, and see what magnificent donations they received! They honored him with libations of whiskey, which they drank themselves. That was all they would give him. The devotion of the Scotch drunkards to their poet is a devotion to their drunkenness, not to him. Doubtless there are many true-hearted men who bewail the sinner as much as they admire the genius, but the masses like him none the worse for his faults. However, if it had been ordained and decreed that every drunkard who honored Burns should go without his whiskey for a week, there would not have been a dozen of them would have done it—not even a half-dozen. Their honor to him was an honor to themselves. It was an opportunity for drunkenness, at least in thousands of instances.

As I stood by his monument some time ago, I saw around it a most dismal, dingy display of withered flowers. I thought, So this is his honor! O Burns! How have you spent your life to have a withered wreath for the world's payment of a life of mighty genius and a flood of marvelous song! Yes, when the world pays best she pays nothing, and when she pays least, she pays her flatterers with scorn. She rewards their services with neglect and poverty.

Many a statesman might I quote who has spent his life in the world's service, and at first the world said, "Go on, go on," and he was applauded everywhere. He was doing something to serve his time. However, he made a little mistake—a mistake, perhaps, which may prove not to have been a mistake at all when the books of history shall be read with a clearer eye. "Down with him!" says the world, "We will have nothing more to do with him." All he may have done before means nothing. One mistake, one flaw in his political career, and he hears, "Down with him! Cast him to the dogs. We will have nothing to do with him again." Ah, the world pays scantily indeed!

What will it do for those it loves the best? When it has done all it can, the last resource of the world is to give a man a title (and what is that)? Then it gives him a tall statue, set up there to bear all weather, to be pitilessly exposed to every storm. There he stands for fools to gaze at, one of the world's great ones paid in stone. It is true the world has paid that out of its own heart, for that is what the world's heart is made of.

The world pays scantily. But did you ever hear a Christian who complained thus of his Master? "No," will he say, "when I serve Christ, I feel that my work is my wages, that labor for Christ is its own reward. He gives me joy on earth, with a fullness of bliss hereafter." Oh, Christ is a good paymaster! *The wages of sin is death, but the gift of God is eternal life in Jesus Christ our Lord"* (Romans 6:23). He that serves Christ may get but little gold and silver such as this world calls precious, but he gets a gold and a silver that shall never be melted in the last refining fire, that shall glitter among the precious things of immortality throughout eternity. The world pays niggardly and scantily, but Christ does not.

If you will serve the world and wish to have gifts from it, the world will pay you half-heartedly. By the world, I mean the religious world as much as any other part of it. I mean the whole world—religious, political, good, bad, and indifferent—the whole lot of them. If you serve the world, it will pay you half-heartedly. Let a man spend himself for his fellow-creatures' interests. What will he get for it? Some will praise him; some will abuse him. The men that escape without abuse in this world are the men who do nothing at all. He who is most valiant and useful must expect to be most reprobated and abhorred.

Those men who are borne upon the waves of popular applause are not the men whose worth is true. Real philanthropists must swim against the stream. The whole list of the world's benefactors is an army of martyrs. All along, the path of the good is marked with blood and fire. The world does not pay the men that serve it really, except with ingratitude. I say again, even when the world does pay, it pays half-heartedly.

Did you ever know a man yet concerning whom the world's opinion was singular? I never heard of any. "Oh," says one, "So-and-so is one of the best men of his times!" Go down the next street, and you will hear it said, "He is the biggest vagabond living." Go to one, and you will hear him say, "I never heard a man of such genius as that is." "Oh," says another, "mere twaddle!" "There is such a newspaper," says one, "how ably it defends the rights of the people!" "Oh," says another, "mere democracy, seeking to pull down everything that is constitutional and proper!"

The world never made up its mind about any man yet. There is not a soul living concerning whom the world is unanimous. But when Christ gives anything, He always gives with all His heart. He does not say to His people, "There, I give you this, but still I have half a mind to keep it back." No, Christ gives His heart to all His people. There is no double-mindedness in Jesus. If we are enabled by free grace to serve Him and to love Him, we may rest quite sure that in the rich reward which His grace shall give us, His whole heart shall go with every blessing. When Christ blesses the poor needy soul, He does not give with one hand and strike with the other. Instead, He gives him mercies with both His hands—both full. He asks the sinner simply to receive all that He is willing to give.

Whenever the world gives anything, it gives mostly to those who do not want it. I remember once, about having a dog which I very much prized when I was a lad, and some man in the street asked me to give him the dog. I thought it was pretty impudent, and I said as much. However, a gentleman to whom I told it said, "Now suppose 'the Duke' (who was a great man in the neighborhood) asked you for the dog. Would you give it him?" I said, "I think I would." He said, "Then you are just like all the world. You would give to those who do not want."

Who would object to give anything to the Queen? Not a soul of us. And yet, perhaps, there is no person in the world who so little needs our gifts. We can always give to those who do not require anything, for we feel that there is some small honor conferred upon us—an honor bestowed by the reception of the gift.

Now, look at Jesus. When he gives to His friends, He gets no honor from them. The honor is in His own free heart which leads Him to give to such poor necessitous worms. Great men have gone to Christ with mere professions and have asked Him to be good to them. But then they have, at the same time, declared that they had a righteousness of their own and did not want Him. He has sent them about their business and given them nothing. He said, *"I have not come not to call the righteous, but sinners, to repentance"* (Luke 5:32). But whenever poor, lost sinners have gone to

Christ, He has never turned one of them away—never. He has given all they could possibly want and infinitely more than they thought they could ever expect. Might not Jesus say to us, when we ask Him for the blessings of His grace, "You are impudent in daring to ask"? But instead of that, He loves to be asked, and He freely and richly gives, *not as the world gives* (John 14:27). He gives to those who need it most.

There is another view of the world's gifts. The world gives to its friends. Any man will help his own friends. If we help not our own relatives and friends, then are we worse than heathen men and publicans. But the world generally confines its good wishes and blessings to its own class, close friends, and relatives. It cannot think of giving blessings to its enemies. Did you ever hear yet of the world's blessing an enemy? Never. It gives its benefactions to its friends, but very scantily even to them.

However, Christ gives his benefactions even to His enemies. *"Not as the world gives,"* He may truly say. The world says, "I must see whether you deserve it. I must see that your case is a good one." It inquires and inquires and inquires again. But Christ only sees that our case is a bad

144

one, and then He gives. He wants not a good case, but a bad case. He knows our need. Once discovering our necessity, not all our sin can stop the hand of His bounty. Oh, if Jesus should call to mind some of the hard speeches we have uttered about Him, He would never bless us, surely, if it were not that His ways are far above our ways. (See Isaiah 55:7-9.) Why, remember, man, it is not long ago since you cursed Him, since you laughed at His people, despised His ministers, and could spit upon His Bible. Jesus has cast all that behind His back and loved you notwithstanding.

Would the world have done that? Let a man get up and rail at his fellows, will they forgive? And, if they forgive, will they begin to bless afterwards? Will they die for their enemies? Oh, no! Such a thing never entered into the heart of man. But Christ blesses rebels, traitors, enemies to His cross. He brings them to know His love and taste of His eternal mercies.

The world always gives with a sparing motive. Most of us are compelled to economy. If we give anything away to a poor man, we generally hope that he will not come again. If we give him half-a-crown, it is very often just to get rid of him. If we bestow a little charity, it is in the hope that we will not see his face soon, for really we do not like the same men begging continually at our door when the world is so full of beggars.

Did you ever hear of a man who gave a beggar something to encourage him to keep on begging from him? I must confess I never did such a thing and am not likely to begin. But that is just what Christ does. When He gives us a little grace, His motive is to make us ask for more. When He gives us even more grace, it is given with the very motive to make us come and ask again. He gives us silver blessings to induce us to ask for golden mercies. When we have golden favors, those same mercies are given on purpose to lead us to pray more earnestly and open our mouth wider so that we may receive more.

What a strange giver Christ is! What a strange friend, that He gives on purpose to make us beg for more! The more you ask of Christ, the more you can ask. The more you have received, the more you will want. The more you know Him, the more you will desire to know Him. The more grace you receive, the more grace you will pant after. When you are full of grace, you will never be content till you get full of glory. Christ's way of giving is, *"Of His fullness we have all received, and grace for grace"* (John 1:16). This is grace to make us pant for more grace—grace to make us long after something higher, something fuller and richer still. *"Not as the world gives, give I unto you."*

21

The King and the Bishop

How man has struggled against man! Man is the wolf of mankind. Not the elements in all their fury, nor the wild beasts of prey in all their cruelty, have ever been such terrible enemies to man as man has been to his own fellow. When you read the story of the Marian persecution in England, you are astounded that ever creatures wearing a human form could be so bloodthirsty. Call these Catholics who thus persecuted the Protestants? Call them Catholics? Much better call them cannibals, for they behaved more like savages than Christians, in their bloody martyrdoms and murders of the saints of God.

We do not in this age feel the cruelty of man to that extent, but this is only because the custom of the land will not allow it. Now there are many who would not dare strike with the hand, but who are very busy in lashing out with their tongues. This is not by exposing our errors, which they have a perfect right to do. Rather, in many cases, the children of God are misrepresented, slandered, persecuted, abused, and ridiculed for truth's sake. We know many instances in which other means have been used—anything to drive the servants of God away from their integrity and from their simple following of their Master. Well did the Lord Jesus say, *"Beware of men... Behold, I send you forth as sheep in the midst of wolves. Therefore, be wise as serpents and harmless as doves"* (Matthew 10:17, 16).

Do not expect men to be the friends of your piety, or if they are, suspect the reality of that piety of which ungodly man is a friend. You must expect to be sometimes bullied and sometimes coerced, to be sometimes flattered and then threatened. You must expect at one time to meet with the oily tongue which has under it the drawn sword, and at another time with the drawn sword itself. Look out, and expect that men will be against you. But what are they all?

Suppose every living man in the world were against you and that you had to stand in solitude like Athanasius, you might say, as he did, "I, Athanasius, against the whole world. I know I have truth on my side, and therefore against the world I stand."

Of what use was the malice of men against Martin Luther? They thought to burn him, but he died in his bed despite them all. They thought to put an end to him, but his little tracts went everywhere. The words of Luther seemed to be carried on the wings of angels, until in the most distant places the Pope found an enemy suddenly springing up where he thought the good seed had all been destroyed.

I do not know that it is of any very great service to have numbers with you. I question whether truth has not generally to be with the minority, and whether it is not quite as honorable to serve God with two or three as it would be with two or three million. If numbers could make a thing right, idolatry ought to be the right religion. If, in countries across the sea, numbers made the idea right, those who fear the Lord would be few indeed, and idolatry and Romanism would be the right thing. Never judge according to numbers. Say they are nothing but men after all. If there are good men fighting on your side, but if they and the truth fall out, fall out with them. Be a friend to the truth. Make your appeal to the law and to the testimony. If others speak not according to this word, it is because there is no light in them.

That was grand of Latimer, when he preached before Henry VIII. He had greatly displeased his majesty by his boldness in a sermon preached before the king, and was ordered to preach again on the following Sabbath, and to make an apology for the offence he had given. After reading his text, the bishop thus began his sermon: "Hugh Latimer, do you know before whom you are this day to speak? To the high and mighty monarch, the king's most excellent majesty, who can take away your life if you offend. Therefore, take heed that you speak not a word that may displease. But then, consider well, Hugh. Do you not know from whence you come, upon whose message you are sent? Even by the great and mighty God, who is all-present, and who beholds all your ways, and who is able to cast your soul into hell! Therefore, take care that you deliver your message faithfully." He then proceeded with the same sermon he had preached the preceding Sabbath, but with considerably more energy.

Such courage should all God's children show when they have to deal with man. You are yourself nothing but a worm. But if God puts His truth into you, do not play the coward, or stammer out His message, but stand up manfully for God and for His truth.

Some people are forever crying for what they call a becoming modesty. Modesty is very becoming, but an ambassador of God must recollect there are other virtues besides modesty. If Her Majesty sent an ambassador to a country with whom we were at war, what would happen if the little man should step into the conference and say, "I humbly hope you will excuse my being here. I wish to be in all things compliant to your honors and lordships, the plenipotentiaries. I feel I am a young man, and you are much older than I am. Therefore I cheerfully submit my judgment to your superior wisdom and experience"? Why, I am sure Her Majesty would command him back again and then into a long retirement.

What business has he to humble himself when he is an ambassador for the Queen! He must remember he is clothed with the dignity of the power which sent him. Even so is God's minister, and he should count it as shameful to stoop to any man. He takes for his motto, *Cedo nulli*, "I yield to none." Preaching God's truth in love and honesty, he hopes to be able to render a fair account to his Master at last, for unto his Master only does he stand or fall.

22

Talents Great and Small

"Well done, good and faithful servant; you were faithful over a few things, I will make you ruler over many things. Enter into the joy of your Lord." —Matthew 25:21, 23

Here comes Whitefield, the man that stood before twenty thousand people at a time to preach the gospel, who in England, Scotland, Ireland, and America, has testified the truth of God, and who could count his converts by thousands, even with one sermon! Here he comes, the man that endured persecution and scorn and yet was not moved—the man of whom the world was not worthy, who lived for his fellowmen and died at last for their cause. Stand by, angels, and admire, while the Master takes him by the hand and says, *"Well done, well done, good and faithful servant:*

enter into the joy of your Lord." See how free grace honors the man whom it enabled to do valiantly!

Hark! Who is this that comes here? A poor, thin-looking creature, who on earth was a consumptive. There was a hectic flush now and then upon her cheek, and she lay three long years upon her bed of sickness. Was she a prince's daughter, for it seems heaven is making much stir about her? No, she was a poor girl who earned her living by her needle, and she worked herself to death! Stitch, stitch, stitch, from morning to night! Here she comes. She went prematurely to her grave, but she is coming, like a shock of fully ripe corn, into heaven. Her Master says, *"Well done, good and faithful servant: you have been faithful in a few things, I will make you ruler over many things. Enter into the joy of your Lord."*

She takes her place by the side of Whitefield. Ask what she ever did, and you find out that she used to live in some back garret, down some dark alley in London. There used to be another poor girl who came to work with her. That poor girl was a gay and volatile creature when she first came to work with her. This consumptive child told her about Christ. They used to creep out evenings to go to chapel or to church together when she was well enough. It was hard at first to get the other one to go, but she used to press her lovingly. When the girl went wild a little, she never gave her up. She used to say, "O Jane, I wish you loved the Savior." When Jane was not there, she used to pray for her. When she was there, she prayed with her. Now and then while stitching away, she read a page out of the Bible to her, for poor Jane could not read. With many tears she tried to tell her about Jesus, who loved her and gave Himself for her. At last, after many days of hard persuasion, many hours of sad disappointment, and many nights of sleepless, tearful prayer, she lived to see the girl profess her love to Christ.

She left her and took sick. There she lay until she was taken to the hospital, where she died. While she was in the hospital, she used to have a few tracts which she gave to those who came to see her. She would try, if she could, to get the women to come around, and she would give them a tract. When she first went into the hospital, if she could creep out of bed, she would get by the side of one who was dying, and the nurse used to let her do it. At last she became too ill. Then she would ask a poor woman on the other side of the ward, who was getting better and was leaving, if she would come and read a chapter to her. It was not that she wanted her to read to her on her own account, but for the other's sake. She thought it might strike her heart while she was reading it. At last this poor girl died and fell asleep in Jesus. This poor, consumptive needlewoman had said to her, *"Well done."* What more could an archangel have said to her?

See then, the Master's commendation, and the last reward will be equal to all men who have used their talents well. If there are degrees in glory, they will not be distributed according to our talents, but according to our faithfulness in using them. As to whether there are degrees or not, I know not. But this I do know: he that does his Lord's will, shall have said to him, *"Well done, good and faithful servant."*

23

The Light of Evening

If our sun does not go down before, we may all expect to have an evening time of life. Either we shall be taken from this world by death, or else, if God should spare us, we shall arrive at the evening of life.

In a few more years, the dry and yellow leaf will be the fit companion of every man and every woman. Is there anything melancholy in that? I think not. The time of old age, even with all its infirmities, seems to me to be a time of peculiar privilege to the Christian. To the worldly sinner, whose zest for pleasure has been removed by the debility of his powers and the decay of his strength, old age must be a season of tedium and pain. But to the veteran soldier of the cross, old age must assuredly be a time of great blessedness and joy.

I was thinking the other evening, while riding in a delightful country, how like evening time old age is. The sun of hot care has gone down—that sun which shone on our early piety that had not much depth of root, and which scorched it so that it died; that sun which scorched our next true godliness and often made it nearly wither and would have withered it, had it not been planted by the rivers of water—that sun is now set.

The good old man has no particular care now in all the world. He says to business, to the hum, noise, and strife of the age in which he lives, "You are nothing to me now. To make my calling and election sure, to hold firmly this my confidence, and to wait until my change comes—this is all my employment. With all your worldly pleasures and cares, I have no connection." The toil of his life is all done. No more does he have to be sweating and toiling as he did in his youth and manhood. His family have grown up and are no more dependent upon him. It may be God has blessed him so that he has sufficient provision for the wants of his old age, or it may be that in some rustic almshouse he breathes out the last few years of his existence.

Like the laborer who, when he returns from the field in the evening, casts himself upon his couch, so does the old man rest from his labors. At evening time we gather into families. The fire is kindled, the curtains are drawn, and we sit around the family fire, to think no more of the things of the great rumbling world. Even so in old age, the family, and not the world, is the engrossing topic for the elderly patriarch.

Did you ever notice how venerable grandfathers, when they write letters, fill them full of information concerning their children? "John is well," "Mary is ill," or, "All our family are in health." Very likely some business friend writes to say, "Stocks are down," or, "the rate of interest is raised," but you never find that in any good old man's letters. He writes about his family, his lately married daughters, and all that. Likewise, we do the same in the evenings. We think only of the family circle and forget the world. That is what the gray-headed old man does. He thinks of his children and forgets all beside.

Well, then, how sweet it is to think that for such an old man there is light in the darkness! *At evening time it shall be light* (Zechariah 14:7 KJV). Dread not your days of weariness, dread not your hours of decay. O soldier of the cross, new lights shall burn when the old lights are quenched. New candles shall be lit when the lamps of life are dim. Fear not! The night of your decay may be coming on, but *"at evening time it shall be light."*

At evening time the Christian has many lights that he never had before, lit by the Holy Spirit and shining by His light. There is the light of a bright experience. He can look back, and he can raise his own Ebenezer saying, *"Thus far the Lord has helped [me]"* (1 Samuel 7:12). He can look back at his old Bible, the light of his youth, and say, "This promise has been proved to me. This covenant has been proved true. I have thumbed through my Bible many a year, but I have never yet thumbed a broken promise. The promises have all been kept to me. Not one good thing has failed."

Further, if he has served God, he has another light to cheer him. He has the remembrance of the good God has enabled him to do. Some of his spiritual children come in and talk of times when God blessed his conversation to their souls. He looks on his children and his grandchildren rising up to call the Redeemer blessed. At evening time he has a light.

161

However, at the last, the night comes in real earnest. He has lived long enough, and he must die. The old man is on his bed. The sun is going down, and he has no more light. "Throw up the windows, and let me look for the last time into the open sky," says the old man. "The sun has gone down. I cannot see the mountains yonder. They are all a mass of mist. My eyes are dim, and the world is dim too."

Suddenly a light shoots across his face, and he cries, "O daughter! Here! I can see another sun rising. Did you not tell me that the sun went down just now? I see another. Where those hills used to be in the landscape that were lost in darkness, I can see hills that seem like burning brass. I think on that summit I can see a city as bright as jasper. Yes, I see a gate opening and spirits coming forth. What is they say? Oh, they sing! They sing! Is this death?"

Before he has asked the question, he has gone where he needed not to answer it because death is unknown there. Yes, he has passed the gates of pearl. His feet are on the streets of gold. His head is bedecked with the crown of immortality. The palm branch of eternal victory is in his hand. God has accepted him in the Beloved.

24

Beds That Are Too Short

For the bed is too short to stretch out on, and the covering so narrow that one cannot wrap himself in it. —Isaiah 28:20

As to the present world, how many beds are there of man's own invention. One man has made himself a bedstead of gold. The pillars are of silver. The covering is of Tyrian purple. The pillows are filled with down, such as only much fine gold could buy him. The hangings he has embroidered with threads of gold and silver, and the curtains are drawn upon rings of ivory. Lo, this man hath ransacked creation for luxuries and invented to himself all manner of sumptuous delights. He gets for himself broad acres and many lands. He adds house to house and field to field. He digs, he toils, he labors, he is in hopes that he shall get enough, a sufficiency, a satisfactory inheritance. He proceeds from enterprise to enterprise. He invests his money in one sphere of labor and then another. He attempts to multiply his gold until it gets beyond all reckoning. He becomes a merchant prince, a millionaire, and he says to himself, "Soul, relax. Eat, drink, and be merry. You have much goods laid up for many years."

Do you not envy this man his bed? Are there not some of you, whose only object in life is to get such a couch for yourselves? You say, "He has well-feathered his nest. I wish that I could do the same for myself!" Ah! But do you know that his bed is too short for him to be able to stretch himself out on it? If you cast yourself upon it for a moment, the bed is long enough for you, but it is not long enough for him.

I have often thought that many a man's riches would be sufficient for me, but they are not sufficient for him. If he makes them his god and seeks in them his happiness, the man never seems to have enough, for his lands are still too narrow and his estate too small. When he begins to stretch himself out, he finds there is something lacking. If the bed could only be made a little longer, he thinks, then he could be quiet and have room enough. But when the bed is lengthened, he finds he has grown longer, too. When his fortune has grown as big as the bedstead of Og, king of Bashan, even then he finds he cannot lie upon it easily.

We read of one man who stretched himself along the whole world which he had conquered, but he found there was not room enough and began to weep because there were not other worlds to conquer. One would have thought a little province would have been enough for him to rest in. But, so big is man when he stretches himself that the whole world does not suffice. If God should give to the avaricious all the mines of Peru, all the glittering diamonds of Golconda, all the wealth of worlds, and if He were then to transmute the stars into gold and silver and make us emperors of an entire universe till we should talk of constellations as men talk of hundreds and universes as men talk of thousands, even then the bed would not be long enough on which we might stretch our ever-lengthening desires. The soul is wider than creation, broader than space. If given all, it would still be unsatisfied, and man would not find rest.

You say, "That is strange. If I had a little more, I would be very well satisfied." You make a mistake. If you are not content with what you have, you would not be satisfied if it were doubled. "No," says one, "I would be." You do not know yourself. If you have fixed your affection on the things of this world, that affection is like a leech that cries, "Give! give!" It will suck, suck, suck to all eternity and still cry, "Give, give!" Though you give it all, it has not gotten enough. The bed, in fact, *is too short to stretch out on.*

Let us look in another direction. Other men have said, "Well, I do not care for gold and silver. Thank God, I have no avarice." But they have been ambitious. "Oh," says one, "if I might be famous, what would I not do? Oh, if my name might be handed down to posterity, as having done something and having been somebody, a man of note, how satisfied would I be!" And the man has so acted, that he has at last made for himself a bed of honor. He has become famous. There is scarcely a newspaper which does not record his name. His name has become a household word. Nations listen to his voice. Thousands of trumpets proclaim his deeds. He is a man, and the world knows it, stamping him with the adjective *"great."* He is called "a great man." See how soft and downy is his bed! What would some of you give to rest upon it? He is fanned to sleep by the breath of fame, and the incense of applause smokes in his chamber. The world waits to refresh him with renewed flattery. Would you not give your ears and eyes if you might have a bed like that to rest upon?

But did you ever read the history of famous men, or hear them tell their tales in secret? "Uneasy lies the head that wears the crown," even though it is the laurel coronet of honor. When the man is known, it is not enough. He asks for wider praise.

There was a time when the praise of a couple of old women was fame to him. Now the approval of ten thousand is nothing. He talks of men as if they were but flocks of wild asses. What he looked up to once as a high pinnacle is now beneath his feet. He must go higher still, though his head is reeling, his brain is whirling, and his feet are slipping. He has done a great thing: he must do more. He seems to stride across the world. He must leap further yet, for the world will never believe a man is famous unless he constantly outdoes himself. He must not only do a great thing today, but he must do a greater thing tomorrow, the next day a greater feat still, and continue to pile his mountains one upon another until he mounts the very Olympus of the demigods. But, suppose he gets there. What does he say? "Oh, that I could go back to my cottage, that I might be all unknown, that I might have rest with my family and be quiet. Popularity is a care which I never endured until now, a trouble that I never guessed. Let me lose it all, let me go back!" He is sick of it. The fact is that man never can be satisfied with anything less than the approbation of heaven. Until conscience gets that, all the applause of senates and of princes is a bed shorter than a man can stretch himself out on.

There is another bed on which man thinks he could rest. There is a witch, a painted harlot, who wears the richest gems in her ears and a necklace of precious jewels about her neck. She is an old deceiver. She was old and shrivelled in the days of Bunyan. She painted herself then, she paints now, and paint she will as long as the world endures. She gads about, and men think her young and fair, lovely and desirable. Her name is Madam Wanton. She keeps a house in which she feeds men and makes them drunken with the wine of pleasure, which is as honey to the taste, but is venom to the soul. This witch, when she can, entices men into her bed. "There," she says, "there, how daintily have I spread it!" It is a bed, the pillars of which are pleasure. Above is the purple of rapture, and beneath is the soft repose of luxurious voluptuousness. Oh, what a bed! Solomon once laid in it, and many since have sought their rest there. They have said, "Away with your gold and silver. Let me spend it that I may eat, drink, and be merry, for tomorrow I die. I care not for fame. I would sooner have the pleasures of life or the joys of Bacchus, than the laurel of fame. Let me give myself up to the intoxication of this world's delights. Let me be drowned in the burgundy of this world's joys."

Have you ever seen such men as that? I have seen many and wept over them. I know some now. They are stretching themselves on that bed and trying to make themselves happy. Byron is just a picture of such men, though he outdid others. What a bed was that he stretched himself on! Was ever a libertine more free in his vices? Was ever a sinner more wild in his blasphemy? Was ever a poet more daring in his flights of thought? Was ever a man more injurious to his fellows than he? And yet, what did Byron say? There is a verse which tells you what he felt in his heart. The man had all that he wanted of sinful pleasure, but here is his confession:

> "I fly like a bird of the air,
> In search of a home and a rest;
> A balm for the sickness of care,
> A bliss for a bosom unblessed."

Still, Byron did not find it. He had no rest in God. He tried pleasure till his eyes were red with it. He tried vice till his body was sick. He descended into his grave a premature old man. If you had asked him, and he had spoken honestly, he would have said that the bed was too short for him to stretch himself out on.

No, young man, you may have all the vices and all the pleasure and mirth of this metropolis—and there is much to be found—but when you have it all, you will find it does not equal your expectations nor satisfy your desires. When the devil is bringing you one cup of spiced wine, you will be asking him next time to spice it more. He will flavor it to your fiery taste, but you will still be dissatisfied, until, at last, if he were to bring you a cup hot as damnation, it would fall tasteless on your palate. You would say, "Even this is tasteless to me, except in the gall, and bitter wormwood, and fire that it brings."

It is so with all worldly pleasure. There is no end to the perpetual thirst. It is like the opium addict. He uses a little and dreams such strange wonders. He wakes, and where are they? Such dreamers look like dead men when awake, with just animation enough to enable them to crawl along. The next time, to get to their elysium, they must take more opium. Each time they require more and more, and all the while they are gradually going down an inclined plane to their graves. That is the effect of human pleasure and all worldly sensual delights. They only end in destruction. Even while they last, they are not wide enough for our desire. They are not large enough for our expectations, *for the bed is too short to stretch out on.*

Think for a moment of the Christian, and see the picture reversed. I will suppose the Christian at his very worst state, though there is no reason why I should do so. The Christian is not necessarily poor. He may be rich, but let us suppose him poor. He has not a foot of land to call his own. He lives by the day. He lives well, for his Master keeps a good cupboard for him and furnishes him with all he requires. He has nothing in this world except the promise of God with regard to the future. The worldly man laughs at the promise, and says it is good for nothing. Now look at the Christian. He says:

> There's nothing round this spacious globe,
> Which suits my large desires;
> To nobler joys than nature gives,
> Thy servant, Lord, aspires.

"Poor man, are you perfectly content?" "Yes," says he, "it is my Father's will that I should live in poverty. I am perfectly content." "Well, but is there nothing else you wish for?" "Nothing," says he, "I have the presence of God. I have delight in communion with Christ. I know that there is laid up for me a crown of life that fades not away, and more I cannot want. I am perfectly content. My soul is at rest."

25

Mistaken Zeal

Those who have no life nor energy may easily ruin themselves, but they are not likely to harm others. However, a mistaken zealot is like a madman with a firebrand in his hand. Persons who are zealous about a mistaken belief may do such mischief!

What did those scribes and pharisees do in Christ's day? They were very zealous, and under the pressure of their zeal, they crucified the Lord of glory. What did Saul do in his time? He was very zealous. Under the influence of his zeal, he dragged men and women to prison and compelled them to blaspheme. When they were put to death, he gave his voice against them.

I do not doubt that many who burned the martyrs were quite as sincere in their faith as those whom they burned. In fact, it must have taken an incredible amount of sincerity in the case of some to have been able to believe that the cruelties which they practiced were really pleasing to God. We cannot doubt their sincerity, because did not our Lord himself say, *"The time is coming that whoever kills you will think that he offers God service"* (John 16:2)? Documents, written by men who stained their hands with the blood of Protestants, prove that some of them had a right heart towards God. In their mistaken zeal for God, truth, and church unity, they believed that they were crushing out a very deadly error and that the persons whom they sent to prison and to death were criminals that ought to be exterminated because they were destroyers of the souls of men.

Take heed that none of you fall into a persecuting spirit through your zeal for the gospel. A good woman may be intensely zealous, and for that reason she may say, "I will not have a servant in my house who does not go to my place of worship." I have known landlords, wonderfully zealous for the faith, who have turned every Dissenter out of their cottages and have refused to rent one of their farms to a Nonconformist.

I do not wonder at their conduct. If they are zealous and at the same time blind, they will take to exterminating the children of God naturally. Of course, in their zeal, they feel as if they must root out error and schism. They will not have Nonconformity near them, and so they get to work. In their zealous efforts, they hack right and left. They say strong and bitter words and do very cruel things, truly believing that they are doing God service.

They never would think that they are violating the crown rights of God, who alone is Lord of the consciences of men. They would not oppose the will of God if they knew it, and yet they are doing so. They would not willingly grieve the hearts of those whom God loves, and yet they do so when they are browbeating the humble cottager for his faith. They look upon the poor people who differ a little from them as being atrociously wrong. They consider it their duty to set their faces against them.

Under the influence of the zeal that moves them—which is a good thing in itself —they are led to do that which is sinful and unjust. Thus the apostle, after he had felt the weight of the stones from the hands of the Jews, prayed that they might be saved. If they were not, their zeal for God would continue to make them murderers.

Another reason why we long to see the zealous converted is this: because they would be so useful. The man that is desperately earnest in a wrong way, if you can but show him his wrong and teach him what is right, will be just as earnest in the right way. Oh, what splendid Christians some would make who are such devotees of superstition now!

Despite their superstition, I look upon many high churchmen with admiration. Up in the morning early, or at night late, ready to practice all kinds of mortifications, to give their very bodies to be burned and all their substance in alms, ready to offer prayers without number, and to be obedient to rites without end—what more could external religion demand of mortal men? Oh, if we could get these to sit at Jesus' feet and leave the phylacteries and the broad-bordered garments to worship God in spirit and to have no confidence in the flesh, what grand people they would make!

See what Paul himself was, when, counting all he had valued so dear to be but dung, he quit all of it and began to preach salvation by grace alone. While he rushed over the world like a lightning flash and preached the gospel as with a peal of thunder, he loved, lived, and died for the Nazarene whom once in his zeal he had counted to be an impostor.

People should pray with all their might for zealous but mistaken persons, who have a zeal for God, but not according to knowledge. Once more, we are bound to make these people the subject of specially earnest prayer because it is so difficult to convert them. It requires the power of God to convert anybody really, but there seems to be needed a double manifestation of power in the conversion of a downright bigot when his bigotry is associated with dense ignorance and gross error. "Oh," says he, "I do that which is right. I am strict in my religion. My righteousness will save me." You cannot get him out of that. It is easier to get a sinner away from his sin than a self-righteous man out of his self-righteousness.

Conceit of our own righteousness sticks to us as the skin to the flesh. The leopard may sooner lose his spots than the proud man his self-righteousness. Oh, that righteousness of ours! We are so fond of it. Our pride hugs it. We do so like to think that we are good, that we are upright, that we are true, that we are right in the sight of God by nature. Though we may be beaten out of it with many stripes, our tendency is always to return to it. Self-righteousness is bound up in the heart of a man as much as folly in the heart of a child. Though you crush a fool in a mortar among wheat with a pestle, yet his self-righteous folly will not depart from him. He will insist that, after all, he is a good fellow and deserves to be saved. We must, therefore, in a very special manner pray for such, seeing that self-righteousness is a deep ditch, and it is hard to draw him out who has once fallen into it.

Prejudice, of all other opponents, is one of the worst to overcome. The door is locked. You may knock as long as you like, but the man will not open it. He cannot. It is locked, and he has thrown away the key. You may tell him, "You are wrong, good friend," but he is so comfortably assured he is right that all your telling will only make him more angry at you for attempting to disturb his peace. O God! Who but You can draw a man out of this miry clay of self-righteousness? Therefore we cry to You, of your great grace, to do it.

For these and many other reasons, those who have a zeal for God, but not according to knowledge, must have a chief place in our urgent prayers.

26

Selfish Ease

What is this sin about which the Spirit of God said by Moses, *"Be sure your sin will find you out"* (Numbers 32:23)? A learned cleric has delivered a sermon about the sin of murder from this text, another on theft, another on falsehood. Now they are very good sermons, but they have nothing to do with this text, if it is read as Moses uttered it. If you take the text as it stands, there is nothing in it about murder, theft, or anything of the kind.

In fact, it is not about what men do, but it is about what men do not do. The iniquity of doing nothing is a sin which is not so often spoken of as it should be. A sin of omission is clearly aimed at in this warning, *"If you do not do so...be sure your sin will find you out."*

What, then, was this sin? Remember that it is the sin of God's own people. It is

179

not the sin of Egyptians and Philistines, but the sin of God's chosen nation. Therefore this text is for you that belong to any of the tribes of Israel—you to whom God has given a portion among His beloved ones. It is to you, professed Christians and church members, that the text comes, *"Be sure your sin will find you out."* And what is that sin? Sadly, it is common among professed Christians and needs to be dealt with: it is the sin which leads any to forget their share in the holy war which is to be carried out for God and for his church.

A great many wrongs are tangled together in this crime, and we will try to separate them and set them in order before your eyes. First, it was the sin of idleness and of self-indulgence. "We have cattle. Here is a land that yields much pasture. Let us have this for our cattle. We will build folds for our sheep with the abundant stones that lie about. We will repair these cities of the Amorites and dwell in them. They are nearly ready for us, and there our little ones will dwell in comfort. We do not care about fighting. We have seen enough of it already in the wars with Sihon and Og. Reuben would rather abide by the sheep folds. Gad has more delight in the bleating of the sheep and in the folding of the lambs in His bosom than in going forth to battle."

Alas, the tribe of Reuben is not dead, and the tribe of Gad has not passed away! Many who are of the household of faith are equally indisposed to exertion, equally fond of ease. Hear them say, "Thank God we are safe! We have passed from death unto life. We have named the name of Christ. We are washed in His precious blood, and therefore we are secure." Then, with a strange inconsistency, they permit the fleshly evil of craving carnal ease. They cry, "Soul, you have much laid up for many years, so eat, drink, and be merry."

Spiritual indulgence is a monstrous evil, yet we see it all around. On Sunday these loafers must be well fed. They look out for such sermons as will feed their souls. The thought does not occur to these people that there is something else to be done besides eating. Soul-saving is pushed into the background. The crowds are perishing at their gates. The multitudes with their sins defile the air. The age is getting worse and worse, and man, by a process of evolution, is evolving a devil. Yet these people want pleasant things preached to them. They eat the fat and drink the sweet, they crowd to the feast of fat things full of marrow and of well-refined wines.

Spiritual festivals are their delight: sermons, conferences, Bible studies, and so forth are sought after, but regular service in ordinary ways is neglected. Not a hand's turn will they do. They gird on no armor, they grasp no sword, they wield no sling, they throw no stone. No, they have gotten their possession. They know they have and sit down in carnal security, satisfied to do nothing. They neither work for life, nor from life. They are sluggards, as lazy as they are long. Nowhere are they at home except where they can enjoy themselves and take things easy. They love their beds, but the Lord's fields they neither plow nor reap. This is the sin pointed out in the text, *"If you do not do so, then take note, you have sinned against the LORD; and be sure your sin will find you out."*

The sin of doing nothing is about the biggest of all sins, for it involves most of the others. The sin of sitting still while your brethren go to war breaks both tables of the law and has in it a huge idolatry of self, which neither allows love to God or man. Horrible idleness! God save us!

27

"Be Sober"

Be sober" (1 Peter 1:13). Does not that mean, first, moderation in all things? Do not be so excited with happiness as to become childish. Do not grow intoxicated and delirious with worldly gain or honor. On the other hand, do not be too depressed with passing troubles. There are some who are so far from moderation in sobriety that, if a little goes wrong with them, they are ready to cry, "Let me die." Oh, no.

"Be sober." Keep the middle way; hold to the golden mean. There are many persons for whom this exhortation is most needed. Are there not men around us who blow hot today and cold tomorrow? Their heat is torrid; their cold, arctic. You would think they were angels from the way they talk one day, but you might think them angels of another sort from the manner in which they act at other times. They are up

so high or down so low that in each case they are extreme. Today they are carried away with this, and the next carried away with that.

I knew very well a Christian man to whom I was accustomed to use one salutation whenever I saw him. He was a good man, but changeable. I said to him, "Good morning, friend! What are you now?" He was once a valiant Armenian, setting young people right as to the errors of my Calvinistic teaching. A short time after, he became exceedingly Calvinistic himself and wanted to screw me up several degrees, but I declined to yield. Soon he became a Baptist and agreed with me on all points, so far as I know. This was not good enough, and therefore he became a Plymouth Brethren. After that, he went to the church from which he originally set out. When I next met him I said, "Good morning, brother, what are you now?" He replied, "That is too bad, Mr. Spurgeon. You asked me the same question last time." I replied, "Did I? But what are you now? Will the same answer do?" I knew it would not.

I would earnestly say to all such people, *"Be sober. Be sober."* It cannot be wise to stagger all over the road in this fashion.

Make sure of your footing when you stand. Make doubly sure of it before you shift.

To be sober means to have a calm, clear head, to judge things after the rule of right and not according to the rule of mob. Be not influenced by those who cry loudest in the street, or by those who beat the biggest drum. Judge for yourselves as men of understanding. Judge as in the sight of God with calm deliberation.

"Be sober." That is, be clear-headed. The man who drinks, and thus destroys the sobriety of his body, is befogged and muddled and has lost his way. Ceasing to be sober, he makes a fool of himself. Do not commit this sin spiritually. Be specially clear-headed and calm as to the things of God. Ask that the grace of God may so rule in your heart that you may be peaceful and serene, not troubled with idle fear on one side or with foolish hope on the other.

"Be sober," says the apostle. You know the word translated *"be sober"* sometimes means *"be watchful."* Indeed there is a great kinship between the two things. Live with your eyes open. Do not go about the world half asleep. Many Christians are asleep. Whole congregations are asleep. The minister snores theology, and the

people in the pews nod in chorus. Much
sacred work is done in a sleepy style. You
can have a Sunday School, and teachers
and children can be asleep. You can have a
tract-distributing society with visitors
going around to the doors all asleep. You
can do everything in a dreamy way if so it
pleases you. But says the apostle, "Be
watchful, be alive." Brethren, look alive. Be
so awakened up by these grand arguments
with which we have plied you already, that
you will brace yourselves and throw your
whole strength into the service of your
Lord and Master.

Finally, let us *"hope to the end"* (1 Peter
1:13 KJV). Never despair. Never even doubt.
Hope when things look hopeless. A sick
and suffering brother rebuked me the other
day for being downcast. He said to me, "We
ought never to show the white flag, but I
think you do sometimes." I asked him what
he meant, and he replied, "You sometimes
seem to grow despondent and low. Now I
am near death, but I have no clouds and no
fears." I rejoiced to see him so joyous and
answered, "You are right, my brother.
Blame me as much as you please for my
unbelief, for I richly deserve it." "Why," he
said, "you are the spiritual father of many

186

of us. Did you not bring me and my friend over yonder to Christ? If you get low in spirit after so much blessing, you ought to be ashamed of yourself." I could say nothing other than, "I am ashamed of myself, and I desire to be more confident in the future."

Brethren, we must hope, and not fear. Be strong in holy confidence in God's word, and be sure that His cause will live and prosper. "Hope," says the apostle, "hope right to the end. Go through with it. If the worst comes to the worst, hope still. Hope as much as ever a man can hope; for when your hope is in God you cannot hope too much."

28

Through Floods and Flames

There are many dear children, both boys and girls, who have not been ashamed in their early days to come forward and confess the Lord Jesus Christ. God bless the dear children! I rejoice in them. I am sure that the church will never have to be ashamed of having admitted them. They, at least, show no cowardice. They take a solemn delight in being numbered with the people of God, counting it an honor to be associated with Christ and His church. Shame on you older ones who still hold back! What ails you, that babes and sucklings are braver than you? By the love you bear to Christ, I charge you: come forth and confess His name among this evil and perverse generation.

Is it true? Then joyfully accept the trial which comes with it. Shrink not from the flames. Settle it in your minds that—by divine grace—no loss, nor cross, nor shame, nor suffering shall make you play the coward. Say, like the holy children, *"We have no need to answer you in this matter"* (Daniel 3:16). They did not cringe before the king and cry, "We beseech you, do not throw us into the fiery furnace. Let us have a consultation with you, O king, that we may arrange terms. There may be some method by which we can please you and yet keep our religion." No! They said:

> *¹⁶We have no need to answer you in this matter.*
> *¹⁷If that is the case, our God whom we serve is able to deliver us from the burning fiery furnace, and He will deliver from your hand, O king.*
> *¹⁸But if not, let it be known to you, O king, that we do not serve your gods, nor will we worship the golden image which you have set up.* (Daniel 3:16-18)

Dear friends, let us be ready to suffer for Christ's sake. Some will say, "Do not be imprudent." It is always prudent to do your duty. We do not have enough nowadays of the virtue nicknamed imprudence. I would like to see a display of old-fashioned imprudence in these cold, calculating, selfish days. Oh, for the days of zeal, the days when men counted not their lives dear to them that they might win Christ! At present, men sit down and reckon what it will cost them to do right, weighing their conduct as a matter of profit and loss. Then they call such wicked calculations prudence. It is sheer selfishness. Do right, if it costs you your life.

Where would England have been if the men who won our liberties in former ages had haggled with the world for gain? If they had saved their skins, they would have lost their souls and ruined the cause of God in England. He loves not Christ who does not love Him more than all things. Oh, for men of principle, who know no loss but loss of faith, and desire no gain except the glory of God! Be this your cry:

"Through floods or flames, if Jesus leads
I'll follow where He goes."

You may lose a great deal for Christ, but you will never lose anything by Christ. You may lose for the present time, but you will gain for eternity. The loss is transient, but the gain is everlasting. You will be a gainer by Christ, even if you have to go to heaven by the way of persecution, poverty, and slander. Never mind the way. The end will make full amends. The treasures of Egypt are mere dross compared with the riches of endless bliss.

If it is true that you are willing thus to follow Christ, reckon upon deliverance. Nebuchadnezzar may put you into the fire, but he cannot keep you there, nor can he make the fire burn you. The enemy casts you into the furnace bound, but the fire will loosen your bonds, and you will walk at liberty amid the glowing coals. You will gain by your losses, you will rise by your down-castings.

Many prosperous men owe their present position to the fact that they were faithful when they were in humble employments. They were honest, and for the moment they displeased their employers, but in the end earned their esteem. When Adam Clarke was apprenticed to a tailor, his master showed him how to stretch the cloth when it was a little short, but Adam could not find in his heart to do it. Such a fool of a boy must be sent home to his mother. His godly mother was glad that her boy was such a fool that he could not stoop to a dishonest trick. You know what he became. He might have missed his way in life if he had not been true to his principles in his youth.

Your first loss may be a lifelong gain. Dear young fellow, you may be fired from your situation, but the Lord will turn the curse into a blessing. If all should go softly with you, you might decline in character. By doing a little wrong, you learn to do yet more and more, so losing your integrity, and with it all hope of ever lifting your nose from the grindstone. Do right for Christ's sake, without considering any consequences, and the consequences will be right enough.

29

Show Your Colors

The fact is, that our Lord requires an open confession as well as a secret faith. If you will not render it, there is no promise of salvation for you, but a threat of being denied at the last. The apostle puts it, *"If you confess with your mouth the Lord Jesus and believe in your heart that has God raised Him from the dead, you will be saved"* (Romans 10:9). It is stated in another place this way, *"He who believes and is baptized will be saved"* (Mark 16:16). That is Christ's way for a person to make public the confession of his faith.

If there is a true faith, there must be a declaration of it. If you are candles and God has lit you, *"Let your light so shine before men, that they may see your good works and glorify your Father which is in heaven"* (Matthew 5:16). Soldiers of Christ must, like her Majesty's soldiers, wear their regimental colors. If ashamed of their regiment's symbols, they ought to be drummed out of the regiment. They who refuse to march in rank with their comrades are not honest soldiers.

The very least thing that the Lord Jesus Christ can expect of us is that we confess Him to the best of our power. If you are nailed up to a cross, I will not invite you to be baptized. If you are fastened to a tree to die, I will not ask you to go into a pulpit and declare your faith, for you cannot. But you are required to do what you can do, namely, to make as distinct and open an avowal of the Lord Jesus Christ as may be suitable in your present condition.

I believe that many Christian people get into a lot of trouble through not being honest in their convictions. For instance, if a man goes into a workshop or a soldier into a barracks, and if he does not fly his flag from the first, it will be very difficult for him to run it up afterwards. But if from the outset he is determined to let them know, he can boldly state, "I am a Christian man, and there are certain things that I cannot do to please you, and certain other things that I cannot help doing, though they displease you." When that is clearly understood, after a while the singularity of the position will be gone, and the man will be let alone. But if he is a little sneaky and thinks that he is going to please the world and Christ too, he is in for a rough time. He may depend upon it. His life will be that of a toad under a harrow or a fox in a dog kennel, if he tries the way of compromise. That will never do.

Come out. Show your colors. Let it be known who and what you are. Although your course will not be smooth, it will certainly be not half so rough as if you tried to run with the hare and hunt with the hounds. That situation is a very difficult piece of business.

The man on the cross came out, then and there, and made as open an avowal of his faith in Christ as was possible. The next thing he did was to rebuke his fellow-sinner. He spoke to him in answer to the ribaldry with which he had assailed our Lord. I do not know what the unconverted convict had been blasphemously saying, but his converted comrade spoke very honestly to him, *"Do you not even fear God, seeing you are under the same condemnation? And we indeed justly, for we receive the due reward of our deeds; but this Man has done nothing wrong"* (Luke 23:40-41).

In these days it is even more needed that believers in Christ should not allow sin to go unrebuked, yet a great many of them do so. Do you not know that a person who is silent when a wrong thing is said or done may become a participator in the sin? If you do not rebuke sin—I mean, of course, on all fit occasions and in a proper spirit —your silence will give consent to the sin, and you will become a party to it. A man who saw a robbery and who did not cry, "Stop thief!" would be thought to be in league with the thief. The man who can hear swearing or see impurity, but never utter a word of protest, may well question whether he is right himself.

"Other men's sins" make up a great item in our personal guilt unless we in any way rebuke them. This our Lord expects us to do. The dying thief did it, and did it with all his heart. Therein he far exceeded large numbers of those who hold their heads high in the church.

30

Keep Your Own Garden

I t is well for a man to see to his cattle,
and look well to his flocks and herds.
However, let him not forget to cultivate
that little patch of ground that lies in the
center of his being. Let him educate his
mind and interact with all knowledge.

On the other hand, let him not forget
that there is another plot of ground called
the heart—the character—which is more
important still. Right principles are spiritual
gold. He that has them and is ruled by
them is the man who truly lives. He does
not have life, whatever else he has, who
has not had his heart cultivated and made
right and pure.

Have you thought about your heart
yet? I do not mean whether you have palpitations! I am no doctor. I am speaking now
about the heart in its moral and spiritual

aspects. What is your character, and do you seek to cultivate it? Do you ever use the hoe upon those weeds which are so plentiful in us all? Do you water those tiny plants of goodness which have begun to grow? Do you watch them to keep away the little foxes which would destroy them? Are you hopeful that there yet may be a harvest in your character which God may look upon with approval?

I pray that we may all look to our hearts. *"Keep your heart with all diligence; for out of it spring the issues of life"* (Proverbs 4:23). Pray daily, *"Create in me a clean heart, O God, and renew a steadfast spirit in me"* (Psalm 51:10). If not, you will go up and down in the world doing a great deal, but when it comes to the end, you will have neglected your noblest nature. Your poor starved soul will die that second death, which is the more dreadful because it is everlasting. How terrible for a soul to die of neglect! How can we escape who neglect this great salvation? If we pay every attention to our bodies, but none to our immortal souls, how shall we justify our folly? God save us from suicide by neglect! May we not have to moan out eternally, *"They made me the keeper of the vineyards, but my own vineyard I have not kept"* (Song of Solomon 1:6).

Now, think of another vineyard. Are not some people neglecting their families? Next to our hearts, our households are the vineyards which we are most bound to cultivate. I shall never forget a man whom I knew in my youth, who used to accompany me at times in my walks to the villages to preach. He was always willing to go with me any evening. I did not need to ask him because he asked himself, until I purposely put him off. He also liked to preach much better than others liked to hear him. He was a man who was sure to be somewhere in the front if he could. Even if you snuffed him out, he had a way of lighting himself up again. He was good-natured and irrepressible. He was, I believe, sincerely earnest in doing good.

But two boys of his were well known to me, and they would swear horribly. They were ready for every vice and were under no restraint. One of them drank himself into a dying state with brandy, though he was a mere boy. I do not believe his father had ever spoken to him about the habit of intoxication, though he certainly was sober and virtuous himself. I had no fault to find with him except this grave fault—that he was seldom at home, was not master of the house, and could not control his children. Neither husband nor wife occupied any place of influence in the household. They were simply the slaves of their children. Their children made themselves vile, and the parents did not restrain them! This brother would pray for his children at the prayer meeting, but I do not think he ever practiced family prayer.

It is shocking to find men and women speaking fluently about religion, and yet their houses are a disgrace to Christianity. I suppose that none of you are as bad as that. But, if it be so, please think about this text: *"They made me the keeper of the vineyards, but my own vineyard I have not kept."* The most careful and prayerful father cannot be held accountable for having wicked sons if he has done his best to instruct them. The most anxious and tearful mother cannot be blamed if her daughter dishonors the family, provided the mother has done her best to train her up in the right way. But, if the parents cannot say that they have done their best, and their children go astray, then they are blameworthy. If any have children but do not know where their boys and girls are, let them go quickly and look them up.

If any readers exercise no parental discipline, nor seek to bring their children to Christ, I do implore them to give up every kind of public work until they have first done their work at home. Has anybody made you a minister, but you are not trying to save your own children? I tell you, sir, I do not believe that God made you a minister. For if He had, He would have begun with making you a minister to your own family. *They made me the keeper of the vineyards.* They ought to have known better than to extend the call, and you ought to have known better than to accept it. How can you be a steward in the great household of the Lord when you cannot even rule your own house?

A Sunday-school teacher, teaching other people's children, and never praying with her own! Is not this a sad business? A teacher of a large class of youths who never has taken a class of his own sons and daughters! Why, what will he do when he lives to see his children plunged into vice and sin and remembers that he has utterly neglected them?

I do not know where this knife may cut, but if it wounds you, I pray that you do not blunt its edge. Do you say that this is "very personal"? It is meant to be personal. If anybody is offended by it, let him be offended with himself and mend his ways. No longer let it be true of any of us, *"They made me the keeper of the vineyards, but my own vineyard I have not kept."*

A Talk about Death

It is the part of a brave man, and especially of a believing man, neither to dread death, nor to pine for it; neither to fear it, nor to court it. Through patience possessing his soul (Luke 21:19), he should not despair of life when hard pressed. He should be always more eager to run his race well than to reach its end.

It is not a work for men of faith to predict their own deaths. These things are with God. How long we shall live on earth we do not know and need not wish to know. We do not have the choosing of the length of our lives. If we had such a choice, it would be wise to refer it back to our God.

"Father, into Your hands I commit My spirit" (Luke 23:46) is an admirable prayer for living as well as for dying saints. To wish to pry between the leaves of the book of destiny is to desire a questionable

privilege. Doubtless we live the better because we cannot foresee the moment when this life shall reach its finish.

Job made a mistake as to the date of his death, but he made no mistake as to the fact itself. He spoke truly when he said, *"I know that You will bring me to death"* (Job 30:23). Some day or other, the Lord will call us from our home above ground *"to the house appointed for all living"* (Job 30:23). I invite you this day to consider this unquestioned truth. Are you startled? Why are you? Is it not very wise to talk about our last hours?

"We want a cheerful theme." Do you? Is not this a cheerful theme to you? It is solemn, but it ought also to be welcome to you. You say that you cannot abide the thought of death. Then you greatly need it. Your shrinking from it proves that you are not in a right state of mind, or else you would take it into due consideration without reluctance. It is a poor happiness which overlooks the most important of facts. I would not endure a peace which could only be maintained by thoughtlessness.

You have something yet to learn if you are a Christian, but yet are not prepared to die. You need to reach a higher state of grace and attain to a firmer and more forceful faith. That you are as yet a babe in grace is clear from your admission that to depart and be with Christ does not seem to be a better thing for you than to abide in the flesh.

Should it not be the business of this life to prepare for the next life, and, in that respect, to prepare to die? But how can a man be prepared for what he never considers? Do you intend to take a leap in the dark? If so, you are in an unhappy condition. I beseech you, as you love your own soul, escape from such peril by the help of God's Holy Spirit.

"Oh," says one, "I do not feel called to think of it." Why, the very autumn season calls you to it. Each fading leaf admonishes you. You will surely have to die. Why not think about the inevitable? It is said that the ostrich buries its head in the sand and fancies itself secure, when it can no longer see the hunter. I can hardly imagine that even a bird could be quite so foolish. I beseech you, do not act with such madness.

If I do not think of death, yet death will think of me. If I will not go to death with meditation and consideration, death will come to me still. Let me, then, meet it like a man. To that end, let me look it in the face. Death comes into our houses and steals away our beloved ones. Seldom do I enter the pulpit without missing some accustomed face from its place. Never a week passes over the church without some of our happy fellowship being caught away to the still happier fellowship above.

Whether we will hear him or not, death is preaching to us each time we assemble in public. Does he come so often with God's message, but we refuse to hear? No, let us lend a willing ear and heart and hear what the Lord God would say to us at all times.

Oh, you that are youngest, you that are fullest of health and strength, I lovingly invite you not to put this subject away from you. Remember, the youngest may be taken away. Early in the life of my boys, I took them to the old churchyard of Wimbledon and had them measure some of the little graves within that enclosure. They found several green hillocks which were shorter than themselves. I tried thus to impress upon their young minds the uncertainty of life. I would have every child remember that he is not too young to die.

Let others know that they are not too strong to die. The stoutest trees of the forest are often the first to fall beneath the destroyer's axe. Paracelsus, the renowned physician of old time, prepared a medicine about which he said that a man who took it regularly would never die except of extreme old age. Yet Paracelsus himself died a young man. Those who think they have found the secret of immortality will yet learn that they are under a strong delusion. None of us can discover a spot where we are out of range of the last enemy. Therefore it would be idiotic to refuse to think of it.

A certain arrogant French duke forbade his attendants ever to mention death in his hearing. When his secretary read to him the words, "The late King of Spain," he turned upon him with contemptuous indignation and asked him what he meant by it. The poor secretary could only stammer out, "It is a title which they take." Yes, indeed, it is a title we shall all take. It will be well to note how it will befit us.

The King of Terrors comes to kings, nor does he disdain to strip the pauper of his scanty flesh. To you, to me, to all he comes. Let us all make ready for his certain approach.